# GIMME!

# GIMME!

## The Human Nature of Successful Marketing

## JOHN HALLWARD

John Wiley & Sons, Inc.

Published by John Wiley & Sons, Inc., Hoboken, New Jersey.
Published simultaneously in Canada.

Wiley Bicentennial Logo: Richard J. Pacifico

This publication is designed to provide accurate and authoritative information in regard to the subject matter covered. It is sold with the understanding that the publisher is not engaged in rendering professional services. If legal, accounting, medical, psychological or any other expert assistance is required, the services of a competent professional person should be sought.

Designations used by companies to distinguish their products are often claimed as trademarks. In all instances where John Wiley & Sons, Inc. is aware of a claim, the product names appear in initial capital or all capital letters. Readers, however, should contact the appropriate companies for more complete information regarding trademarks and registration.

For general information on our other products and services please contact our Customer Care Department within the United States at (800) 762-2974, outside the United States at (317) 572-3993 or fax (317) 572-4002.

Wiley also publishes its books in a variety of electronic formats. Some content that appears in print may not be available in electronic books. For more information about Wiley products, visit our web site at www.wiley.com.

*Library of Congress Cataloging-in-Publication Data:*

Hallward, John, 1961–
    Gimme! The human nature of successful marketing / John Hallward.
        p. cm.
    ISBN-13: 978-0-470-10029-5 (cloth : alk. paper)
    ISBN-10: 0-470-10029-X (cloth : alk. paper)
    1. Advertising—Brand name products. 2. Brand name products—Marketing—Management. 3. Human behavior. I. Title. II. Title: Human nature of successful marketing.
    HF6161.B4H35 2007
    658.8—dc22

                                                                              2006023189

Printed in the United States of America.
10 9 8 7 6 5 4 3 2 1

# WHAT IS THE 90-SECOND
# SUMMARY OF THIS BOOK?

We can apply the insights of how people are genetically wired to making marketing more efficient.

Humans are the consequence of genetic evolution, whether through intelligent design or through random gene mutations (survival of the fittest). Some manifestations of evolution found in all cultures include emotions, habits, memories, desires, moods, thinking, and motivation. We share these characteristics because these are the consequences of our genes. The better we can appreciate these characteristics, understand how we are genetically wired, and why we act the way we do, the better we can advertise and the better we can persuade others.

This book explores some of our evolutionary traits and then shows how one of the world's leading consumer market research firm's databases confirm that advertising and brand marketing follow our evolutionary features. This book shares the lessons we have learned about effective advertising and brand management.

Many brands today are now old and familiar. They are under attack from copycat brands, from lower-price brands, from powerful retailers, and from globalization. At the same time, advertising is fragmenting (and possibly decaying), consumers are becoming less loyal, and market researchers struggle to find answers. The solution for brand managers is neither to cut costs nor to rely on promotional activity. The profitable solution is to innovate in a tangible way, or to add something intangible, or both: to add unique, emotional associations to brands, to enrich brands across the human senses, and to create effective advertising properties. This is where we need insights about how humans are wired, and how we can better leverage the drivers of motivation.

# CONTENTS

Acknowledgments                                          xiii

About the Author, and Why "Gimme!"                       xv

Introduction                                             xvii

## PART I

### TODAY'S MARKETING CHALLENGES AND THE EMOTI-SUASION RESPONSE

**CHAPTER 1**  Problems in (Marketing) Paradise                    3

**CHAPTER 2**  Marketers' Response   17
               Competing on Price?   17
               Innovation Is One Answer   20
               Emotional Brand Appeal Is Another Answer   21
               Be Aware of Overengineering   24
               A Call for More Scientists in Marketing   25

**CHAPTER 3**  The Consequences of Our Genetic Evolution          29
               What Is Evolution?   29
               Intelligent Design and the Anti-Darwin School   32
               We Are the Product of Our Genes   32

CONTENTS

Humans Have Habits   33
Detecting Irregularities   36
Not Too Many Facts   38
Cognitive Dissonance: Conflicting Beliefs   39

CHAPTER 4   Mechanics of the Brain                                   43
Neurons: The Bits and Bytes of the Brain   44
Memory: A Pattern of Firing Neurons   46
Functional Areas of the Brain   47
The Growing Brain   50
Emotions in the Brain   51

CHAPTER 5   Processing Our Senses                                    53
The Entry of a Sense   55
Desensitizing to Stimuli   57
Sensory Deprivation   58
Brand Sensations   59

CHAPTER 6   Putting Memory to Work                                   63
Thinking in Units of Memory   65
Advertising Memory   66
Low Attention Processing of Advertising?   70
Advertising Repetition?   71
Serving Up Simple Advertising Memory Units   73

CHAPTER 7   The Important Role of Emotions                           77
What Are Emotions?   77
Why Do We Have Them?   78
Animals Have Emotions, Too   79
The Emotional Human   79
Emotions and Decision Making: Two Peas in the
   Same Pod   82
Death of the Economically Rational Human   86

CHAPTER 8   Beyond Emotions—to Attitudes                             91
Attitudes and Beliefs   92
Direct or Indirect Route to Forming Attitudes   92
Current Attitudes and Future Decisions   93

Changing Attitudes   94

Appreciating Consumers' Beliefs   95

**CHAPTER 9**   Beyond Attitudes—to Motivation                       99

Maslow and Human Needs   101

Cognitive Style   103

Self-Perception Is a Powerful Force   106

**CHAPTER 10**   Gimme! Gimme!                                      109

Our Hedonistic Tendencies   110

Aspirations   111

Comfort Zones   112

Incentives   113

**CHAPTER 11**   Emoti-Suasion                                      117

Expectancy Theory   118

Triggering   120

The Moody Target   122

## PART II

### LESSONS LEARNED AND FOLLOWING OUR GENETIC WIRING

**CHAPTER 12**   Learning from Ipsos Consumer Research             131

Advertising Is a Business   132

Managing the Odds   133

Branding Matters   134

**CHAPTER 13**   35 Lessons Learned                                137

1. Familiarity Is Key: You Cannot Love Something You
   Do Not Know   137
2. Being Different Offers a Competitive Reason to be
   Chosen   139
3. Be Understood for Your Relevance   140
4. The Quality of the Brand Promise and Consistency, Over
   Time, Drive Desire   141
5. Advertising Can Make a Significant Difference When
   Product Performance Is Similar between Competitive
   Choices   143

# CONTENTS

6. Triggering Is Often the Best Objective for Established Brands   146
7. Popularity: Security in Numbers   146
8. Emotions Add an Extra Dimension Beyond the Rational Elements of Product Features   147
9. Advertising's Role Is to Build Emotional Associations for the Brand's Benefit   152
10. It Is Important to Go Beyond Emotional Response to Self-Perceptions, Aspirations, and Comfort Zones   154
11. Emotional Needs, Wants, and Desires Drive Our Motivations   158
12. Brand Icons, Characters, and Spokespersons Strengthen Brand Equity   161
13. Appealing to Many Different Senses Enriches a Brand   162
14. Being Expensive Is Acceptable Because It Is Value That Matters Most   165
15. Private-Label Retailer Brands and Discount Brands Are Becoming Good Enough and Are Reducing the Relevance of Higher-Priced National Brands   166
16. Creative Is King   168
17. Good Advertising Goes to Work Quickly   169
18. Bad Advertising Rarely Wears In   170
19. Memorable Ads Have Something That Helps Them Stick Out   172
20. Poor Branding Is a Major Problem   173
21. Keep It Simple—and Visual   173
22. Branding Devices Are Worthwhile   174
23. Maintain Consistency Over Time (Be Campaignable), but Make New Messages Obvious   176
24. Evolution, Not Revolution   177
25. Aim for Relevant Differentiation   178
26. Social Proof and "Because"   179
27. Advertise for a Reason: News Is Persuasive   180
28. One Unified Creative Approach Works Best   181
29. One Ad at a Time   183
30. Wear-Out—It Happens   184

31. Better Media Planning Can Pay Off    185

32. Share of Voice Is Less Important than Most Marketers
Think    188

33. Recency Planning Is Effective    188

34. Reach Is the Key Element after Creative    190

35. Media Consumption Does Not Match with Ad
Recall    192

**CHAPTER 14** Closing Thoughts                                         197

Evolution at Work: A Case in Point    198

Brand Management Is about Managing to the Emotional
Gimmes    198

It Is Not about Emotional Advertising    200

Differentiation or Domination?    202

Screening for Better Ads    203

Enough Said    205

Glossary                                                                  207

Bibliography                                                              209

Index                                                                     211

# ACKNOWLEDGMENTS

Writing a book takes time and requires sacrifices. I would like to formally thank my wife, Karma, for allowing me the time away from our three young teenagers to write this book. And for my kids, Derek, Evan, and Laura, whose favorite question was "When will the book be finished?"—Very soon!

There are also many others to thank for their guidance, encouragement, comments, and support. Two heads are often better than one, and I could not have done this alone. Thank you to Kevin Ford, who encouraged me to contemplate writing a book and then offered much feedback, food for thought, and guidance; Maria Iliakis, my second brain in our Ipsos offices; Maria had the confidence to be honest in her opinions. This was constructive, reassuring, and much appreciated.

To Erin Williams, who spent hours upon hours editing this book; grammar and spelling were never strong points for me, and Erin has made this read much better. And to the many Ipsos colleagues who have contributed in their own way: Alan Liberman, Alex Gronberger, Bernie Malinoff, Dan Maceluch, Joanne Benson, Tim Keiningham, Tina Calles, and Wendy Swiggett.

Last, but certainly not least, my agent, Michael Ebeling. I started this initiative without any publishing experience. None. Michael explained and looked after everything related to the success of getting a book published.

I must add that if this book is judged to be of any value it is because I am standing on the shoulders of giants. Many great thinkers and writers have written mind-opening books related to our genetic evolution, how our minds work, how consumers think, how our senses contribute, and so on. At the end of this book, I list the authors that I found to be useful and insightful. Maybe you will, too.

It is also important to absolve Ipsos, and all Ipsos people, business units, partners, and so on from any responsibilities or liabilities of this book. I have undertaken the challenge of writing this book by myself, and I take this responsibility as a private individual.

# ABOUT THE AUTHOR, AND WHY "GIMME!"

Why do our knees bend one way while the knees of some shore birds bend the other way? Many years ago, I watched a show with George Carlin, the comedian. He was contemplating the human body and why it worked the way it did. He wondered aloud what a chair would look like if our knees didn't bend down. He also asked why our nose is located in the middle of our face, where everyone can see it. He feels noses are ugly. He added that it gets worse: our noses are upside down, such that runny noses empty right into our mouth. What a mess! Instead, George suggested that noses should be out of the way, like where our belly buttons are located. He then went on to say this would create quite a sight when two Eskimos wanted to kiss by rubbing noses . . . they would have to drop their pants!

For the longest time, I have been curious about why we are the way we are. Why is our nose upside down, right above our mouth? Why do our knees bend one way instead of the other? The answers to such questions allow us to understand ourselves better. This approach of trying to understand humans is the basis of Part 1 of this book. By understanding how we work, we can better understand how to motivate others. This book focuses on motivation, whether it is related to advertising on a large scale or one-to-one with a friend or child, to make us wiser as to what manipulates us.

Why me? The quick answer is because I am a curious ordinary layman and because I am a consumer market researcher. The good news is that I am not a psychologist, neurologist, or medical doctor, so I am going to keep the findings quite straightforward for all to understand. My career spans more than 20 years of conducting consumer surveys dedicated to understanding how advertising affects people and why they buy the brands they do. I have worked on the manufacturer side at Procter & Gamble as well as at Johnson & Johnson. These are two large, established, successful firms interested in understanding how to market their brands to consumers efficiently. Those early days were followed by fourteen years as an owner/manager of a market research firm specializing in consumer advertising and brand equity measurement. Then, in 2000, my partner and I sold our firm to Ipsos, one of the top global market research companies in the world. Today, I continue at Ipsos, specializing in understanding motivation, how advertising persuades, and how consumers are motivated to select one brand over another. As part of such a large and successful organization as Ipsos, I have access to huge databases of advertising (tens of thousands of consumer surveys) and the use of annual R&D budgets to explore consumers' behavior. This book shares some of the leading-edge consumer insights from my cumulative learning and the work at Ipsos.

I have chosen to write this book to help clarify and bring together my own thinking. The concept of writing a book forces the author to organize and clarify his or her thoughts in a manner that can be explained to others. In turn, this is helpful to me. I also write this book in the hope that it helps others to learn things that have taken me decades to acquire. I also smile when I consider that this book will help to explain to family members, neighbors, and friends what I do for a living. I hope readers will better understand important concepts of advertising, of brand management, of consumer research, and of themselves as a member of our species. Personally, I have gained a better appreciation of dealing with others by better understanding how we tick. I hope you do, too.

# INTRODUCTION

I contemplated titling this book *Monkeys, Minds, Moods, and Motivations* because I believe (and evidence supports) that our genetic biologic composition explains how and why we act as we do today. Although we did not directly evolve from monkeys, we do share common ancestors. Humans are a reflection of and a product of our genetic evolution, and by understanding our genetic makeup, we understand our motivations better. All humans, in all cultures across the globe, have common characteristics, such as short-term memory, long-term memory, habits, emotions, and so on. We all have these features, and they come from our DNA and genes; they are genetic. By recognizing these human characteristics and by understanding them better, advertisers (motivators) can develop more effective marketing plans—or at least, advertisers can address these important features instead of ignoring them due to a lack of insight. I have often felt in my marketing career, objectively reviewing advertising as a market researcher, that advertisers ignore the basic facts about how humans are wired and how we work emotionally. It is for these reasons that I like the reference to monkeys. Genetic evolution offers a powerful explanation to our motivations.

Beyond monkeys, our minds, moods, and motivations drive our future behavior. I refer to behavioral psychology, with such aspects as Maslow's hierarchy of needs, self-perceptions, expectancy theory, and other useful insights that explain human actions. Influencing behavior is the goal of marketing, which makes the cash register ring. To be specific, the goal of marketing is not to communicate or to generate emotional advertising. The role of marketing is to drive behavior that generates sales. In a sense, behavioral psychology explains our future while genetic evolution explains our past. There is much to gain by learning some of the insights from behavioral psychologists, and our Ipsos databases support their implications.

Instead of using the title *Monkeys, Minds, Moods, and Motivation*, I settled on *Gimme!* I felt *Gimme!* captured the true essence of human motivation. To a major degree, at the core of human decision making, we feel a desire to choose outcomes that yield pleasing feelings for ourselves. That is, we are motivated to do things that fulfill our own emotional desires. This is a genetic characteristic, and these *gimmes* manifest themselves right from childhood. This brings to mind a rhyme used when our children were younger:

> "Gimme, gimme never gets.
> Don't you know your manners yet?"

We are born with the gimmes, and we are taught to suppress them as we grow up in society, but the gimmes do not go away. The gimmes happen when we choose a brand: "How will I be perceived by using brand X instead of brand Y?" or "What emotional payoffs do I get for choosing brand X over brand Y?" This is how we make our decisions, with the gimmes at the center.

Good selling practices recognize this self-centered focus. Selling of brands or motivating a friend is about catering to the gimmes. Advertisers and people in general can get what they want as an outcome of giving to others what others want. This may be obvious, and nothing new to many, but it is surprising how much advertising is about saying what the advertisers want to say about themselves, failing to focus on the gimmes of the consumer. I often tell my teenage kids to do something (make your bed) based on what I want to see happen rather than thinking about what my teenagers want. I need to get them to make their beds for some reason that appeals to them. People do things better when they want to do it. I refer to this as *emoti-suasion* (the art of persuasion by appealing to peoples' emotional desires). This concept directly recognizes the genetic, self-centered nature of humans. This is the foundation of the art of manipulation.

The simple beauty of emoti-suasion and the gimmes is that these concepts include the many considerations that behavioral psychologists refer to when discussing motivation, such as values, attitudes, moods, self-perceptions, and expectations. Why? Because practically everything we evaluate boils down to our own personal thoughts, personal desires, personal insecurities, personal views of right versus wrong, and personal social interactions with others. We talk to ourselves in our head, and we make decisions based on what we think is best—or what is best based on what meets our emotional needs. It is not only our brain that works on the gimmes, but also our heart, our subconscious, our instincts, and our genetic purpose in life. These are all largely geared toward the self, as we will review in the following chapters.

A quick example may help to clarify the concept of emoti-suasion. A manufacturer of hand drills will try to sell its drills because this is what they do as a business. Consumers do not want drills so much as they want holes in things. This is why we buy drills. But if two or more drill brands make nice holes, how do consumers choose between them? The decision to buy a drill and the choice between brands is likely influenced by the emotional associations related to the brands, the perceptions the consumer wants to experience, and the consumer's emotional desires. Does the consumer choose a brand that implies that he or she is a capable handyman like a true professional or choose a safe-to-use amateur brand? Does the consumer want a sense of self-accomplishment or a nifty brand he or she can show off to the neighbor? Is the brand's image manly or is it perhaps economical? These elements give emotional payoffs (the gimmes) that explain brand choice. Emoti-suasion is about selling a brand that fulfills the emotional needs of consumers. The product features are support points (and likely quite similar between the many brands of drills).

This book also goes well beyond a friendly summary of reflections about the psychology of motivations. As the expression goes: the proof of the pudding is in the eating. Part 2 of this book will review many factual lessons learned from thousands of tested television ads, thousands of tracked advertising campaigns, and thousands of brand equity surveys. Can we find evidence that successful advertising and marketing capitalize on our genetic characteristics? Does advertising work better when it leverages the way humans are wired? In short, the answer is yes. Part 2 of this book is dedicated to finding the factual support within marketing and advertising for effective motivational practices. We will see how well the facts support motivational theories and the genetic explanation of humans. I hope that by sharing the concepts of motivation and then supporting these concepts with observed factual proof, marketers (and people in general) will better learn how to motivate and persuade others and to be aware of such elements as emoti-suasion.

To summarize the flow of this book, we will briefly cover the physical components of humans as these relate to the nervous system, our senses, and our brains. It is within these components that our motivation rests. Fortunately for readers, we do not need to explore the chemistry and biology of the brain fully to learn useful insights about persuasion. We do not need to get too technical. We do not need to know exactly how an automobile works to understand how to drive it, but it does help to know about the gas pedal, brake, and the steering wheel. Then, after the basic physical review of our nervous system, we will review the psychological aspects of human motivations and behavior. With an understanding of these key ideas, we will review the learning from the Ipsos databases of advertising. (Don't worry; this book will avoid excessive details about biology and market research.)

# GIMME!

PART 1

# Today's Marketing Challenges and the Emoti-Suasion Response

# CHAPTER

# 1

# PROBLEMS IN (MARKETING) PARADISE

I FEEL THERE IS A GROWING NEED FOR MARKETERS TO LEARN MORE ABOUT the human gimmes (and about minds, moods, and motivations). The majority of us in marketing, advertising, and sales businesses have a growing challenge for brand management. It is under attack from many fronts. To be defensive, and even opportunistic, we need to respond correctly or many brands run the risk of profit decline.

As a consumer, many of the following observations will feel true. The challenges brand owners face may be liberating to us as shoppers. We do not often stop to consider the nature of our brand choices for deodorant, or batteries, or a bag of sugar. We approach our shopping for many household products in a habitual autopilot manner. If we stop to recognize the issues in the next few pages, some might get a feeling of comfort and even empowerment. We will recognize that each of us is (mostly) in control of our decisions. We can be disloyal, and we can feel free to switch banks, to switch car dealerships for car servicing, and to buy no-name or private-label store brands. Consumers have the power. In turn, marketers must earn consumers' respect and create empathy toward their brands. Perhaps more than ever in the history of shopping, brand owners need to work harder to overcome the many growing challenges.

The following few pages summarize some of the overarching challenges affecting brand management. As I describe these issues, there is a bias toward fast-moving consumer goods (FMCG), because I know these categories best, but I feel (and observe in our data) that these observations also apply to many non-FMCG categories. These challenges should be read in terms of the bigger picture for all of brand management.

## STAGNANT BRANDS

In the past century, particularly from the 1930s to 1980s in the western world, many brands were created by or heavily supported with advertising and sales programs. Consumers became aware and familiar with many (new) brands during this period and exposed their offspring to these brands. In the last 20 to 25 years, many of these big established brands have not really changed other than to add small tweaks to packaging or to add new varieties. I recognize that there have been new modern brand introductions (mainly new technology brands such as PCs, mobile phones, electronic gaming, and so on), but many of the leading personal care brands, grocery brands, household products, and so on have been around for over 25 years. These brands are well known and familiar to consumers. Perhaps too familiar.

## DESENSITIZING

The first problem with this stagnant situation is found in our human nature (our genes). As we will explore later, our human senses, such as taste, smell, touch, and so on, tend to desensitize to familiar old stimuli. As a stimulus continues (for example, the scent of old cigarette smoke in a room), we are genetically wired to pay less attention to it. Our brain unconsciously readjusts our senses to a fresh base zero so we can be ready to detect and process new, unfamiliar stimuli. It is a basic survival trait to be able to desensitize to neutral stimuli. Otherwise, our senses and brain would be overloaded with past and current stimuli, and we would be less capable of detecting new stimuli. Our ancestors, millions of years ago, that did not have this ability to desensitize and to be sensitive to new signs of danger likely died off as weak links in our evolutionary chain.

This concept of desensitizing works to the detriment of established brands. As consumers, we become more passive to familiar, old, mature brands and to established, tired, ongoing ad campaigns. We find supporting evidence for this in our Ipsos databases. Since Ipsos is a leader in advertising research, we have collected thousands of tracked ad campaigns. From these studies, we observe that consumers pay more attention to advertising for new products (and brand extensions) than they do to advertising for mature established products. Figure 1.1 comes from Ipsos' Ad*Graph media model based on thousands of tracked ad campaigns. Notice how campaigns for new products achieve better recall than for established products.

In a similar vein, while attending the 2005 Worldwide Readership Research Symposium in Prague, I was pleasantly surprised to learn more about this point from one particular summary presentation of a small study conducted by the University of Nottingham (commissioned by Bucknull and Masson). This study was about advertising and the involvement of the ad audience for various adverts. Among other findings, one statement caught my attention: "Furthermore, it was found that the more familiar a brand name (to the audience), the less time participants (in the study) spent looking at a particular ad." That is, we appear to spend less time focused on what is already familiar to us.

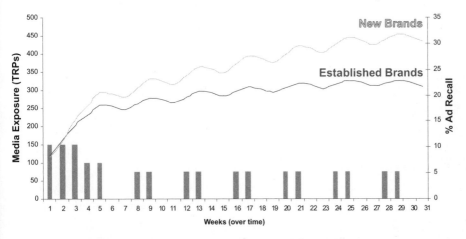

**Fig. 1.1** Ad Recall with New versus Established Brands
*Source:* Ipsos-ASI Ad*Graph Media Model.

To sum up, our genetic evolution leads us to desensitize to familiar stimuli. Old brands that are stagnant and changeless are likely to be taken for granted with little thought. They are disadvantaged compared with newer, dynamic, more engaging brands.

## COPYCAT PRODUCTS AND A PROLIFERATION OF CHOICE

The second problem with stagnant brands appears in the form of copycat or me-too products. As brands become successful, they attract competitors who offer similar products to cash in on the success. Often the copycat products mirror the appearance and the features of the leading brands. Due to our global economy, free trade agreements, and our technologically equipped world, it appears easier and quicker than ever for competitors to copy brand leaders.

In the past 50 years, in many developed countries, there has been an explosion of brand proliferation and consumer choice. It was not so long ago that consumers only had a few brand choices per category in the stores they visited. Today, we have choices among retailers and manufacturers from all corners of the globe, among global brands and local brands, and for the retailers' own private-label brands. So, just as established brands mature, there is a proliferation of brand choice, with many copycat products. The differentiation between products is less and less obvious, and we have (too) many products to consider.

## SUBSTITUTABILITY

It is becoming easy to switch between brands. At Ipsos, we have a proprietary research tool, Equity*Builder, that assesses and quantifies the brand equity and brand health of a brand as perceived by consumers. This is a consumer research tool based on standardized measures, which asks consumers nine questions about how they perceive brands they could buy. To date, in Ipsos databases, we have over four million individual brand assessments, using this same standard set of questions. From this unique robust database we observe a clear indication of the importance of substitutability between brands. Among the nine standard questions in Equity*Builder, one question specifically asks "Is there another brand similar in image or attributes to brand X?" (the brand we are assessing in the survey). Respondents can answer either yes or no. The higher the level of "yes," the greater the challenge to the brand. That is, beyond the specific brand, if there is another competitive brand similar in features or in imagery, then brand loyalty for both brands will be reduced. Consumers can switch between the two or three equally good brands (perhaps choosing the one with the better price). Brand substitutability is a problem for many established brands.

## COMMODITIZATION

As an outcome of these trends, brand marketing seems to be slipping away, and we are observing the increasing commoditization of products and categories. We observe in our Equity*Builder database that in categories where the lower-priced brands are good enough, the relevance of the leading national brands is reduced. In turn, the national independent brands become less competitive and tend to lose their loyal buyers. This loss of advantage is what I refer to as the *commoditization of the category.*

Consider where you shop, and consider how much meaningful difference you feel exists between the top brand choices of bottled water, household batteries, dish detergent, toilet paper, cooking oil, paper towels, plastic food wrap, sugar, flour, window cleaner, bed sheets, light bulbs, garbage bags, and so on, and so on. These products are becoming commodities, with many low-price brands competing well with the leaders.

As leading national brands are squeezed by cheaper copycat products, they feel a need to cut prices to remain competitive. This reduction in prices reduces the gross profit of these national brands and reduces the affordability of their advertising budgets. With less advertising support for brand equity, the appeal of the national brand weakens, particularly for the next generation of shoppers who have no prior brand equity for the brands. The death spiral begins; with less advertising to support the brand, consumers have fewer reasons to buy the brand. The advertiser has to further reduce its higher-price brands to match the low-cost choices. Eventually, the brand has little or no remaining brand equity and is competing mostly on price and distribution.

## THE POWERFUL RETAILERS

Coincidental with the stagnation of many mature brands, and the evolution to commoditization, we observe in almost every continent a growth in the control, dominance, and power of a few retailers (think Wal-Mart as one example). The balance of power is switching away from brand manufacturers, toward the retailers and distribution channels. In turn, these retailers have greater control about where, how, and when the products on their shelves will be merchandised.

Most major retailers have now introduced their own private labels (store brands) to compete with national brands from established, known manufacturers. Several retailers have two levels of store brands: one to be similar (or even better) in quality to the leading national brand, but at a better price, and a second label to be lowest priced. Since the retailers often earn greater profit margins on their own private brands than selling national brands, they will feature their own products over the national brands. These retailers control the shelves, the prices, and the promotional flyers. The retail trade is becoming ever more important to the success or failure of national independent brands. As an example, according to an A. C. Nielsen web site, private-label products account for over 50 percent of packaged grocery expenditures in the United Kingdom.

## DISLOYAL CONSUMERS

With all of these challenges facing marketers and their brands, we find that consumers are also becoming less loyal in most regions of the world. Consumers are gaining confidence as shoppers. We are becoming ever more confident in making our own choices. We are losing our guilt toward buying no-name products or about switching brand loyalties. Even beyond brand loyalty, we are feeling less guilty about channel surfing and skipping TV adds. This guilt-free feeling is found beyond marketing as well. In the last 25 years, we have seen a real increase in divorce rates. We have seen a move away from organized religion in many regions. Workers are more frequently changing jobs, companies, and careers, and we have observed a move toward democracy and capitalism in many previously undemocratic countries. All to say, consumers (and society as a whole) appear to be evolving toward freedom of (guilt free) choice. Perhaps this has been facilitated, encouraged, and even flamed by the Internet and globalization. As well, perhaps this movement toward disloyalty is a natural consequence of the evolution of our developed societies.

When Darwin was writing his books in the mid- to late 1800s, it was risky and perhaps theologically unacceptable to apply the theory of evolution to humans, but more recently, some modern social-Darwinian scientists now argue that this evolution from social group behavior to individualism is genetic. Richard Dawkins, in his book *The Selfish Gene,* discusses the concept of stable environments and how selfish people will take advantage of social groups for their own personal benefit. In turn, social groups that work to the common good of all will be destabilized by selfish individuals, causing an evolution toward individual selfish desires. This appears to be at play worldwide, as communism evolves toward more capitalistic and democratic societies in places such as China and the old Soviet bloc of Eastern Europe. Pure communism is in conflict with our genetic evolution as humans. We are predetermined to be somewhat greedy and to be loyal mostly to our individual self. There is a genetic basis for having greedy, selfish tendencies (this is the basis of survival of the fittest).

## INTERNET SHOPPING

Almost as a paradox to the growing power of a few retailers, the Internet is enabling consumers to stay at home to shop online and find the lowest-cost provider for the products they want. Shopping within the travel industry is being made easy by web sites such as Expedia and Travelocity. Bidding on eBay is an easy way to get the price you want for almost any and every product or brand. The other day, my son wanted to buy a pair of Diesel brand shoes. While downtown (among real brick-and-mortar stores), he visited a store retailing Diesel shoes. He tried on a few pairs to determine the size he needed and found a few of the styles he liked, but he did not buy them. That evening, from the comfort of his home and far from the influence of the retail environment, he went online to buy the new pair of Diesel shoes he wanted, in the size he knew he needed, at a price much lower than at the retailer downtown. The purchase process also works in reverse when consumers first surf the Internet to find what they want and then visit the retail outlet to fill their purchase at the best price. All of this must be a blow to the retail industry. The Internet is a powerful new enabler, and it appears to have escalated the importance of price in the purchase decision.

## MEDIA FRAGMENTATION, ZAPPING, AND ZIPPING

To complicate matters further, the capability of manufacturers and service providers to reach target consumers with meaningful, quality advertising is declining. The traditional advertising media are not working as well as they used to, largely due to emerging digital and entertainment technologies (cable television, personal video recorders, video on demand, the Internet, computer gaming, text messaging, and so on). As one example, an American advertiser in the 1970s used to be able to reach three-quarters of all American adults by placing ads on the three main U.S. television networks. Now, it requires the placement of ads on about 10 times more television channels to reach the same three-quarters of the population. These viewers are more likely than ever to be zipping and zapping right past most of these ad exposures. This ad avoidance is not just restricted to television. We can now purchase advertisement-free satellite radio, and many Internet surfers use software applications to block pop-up ads.

I imagine the same trends are happening in almost all regions of the world (albeit perhaps not at the same fragmented level as found in the United States). In turn, it is becoming harder to reach consumers with advertising messages. So, just as brands need greater love and support, advertising is becoming more challenging for ad agencies.

## ADVERTISING CAMPAIGNS OFTEN FAIL

Another problem directly related to advertising is that it is not easy to create efficient, effective advertising. What do you say that is exciting and fresh for a brand that most consumers have known for 20 or more years? The consumer research databases at Ipsos show that only about one-fifth of advertising campaigns have a significant, observable impact on the brand (in terms of achieving the objectives for advertising). There is debate about the definition of successful advertising, but I am not aware of any studies or

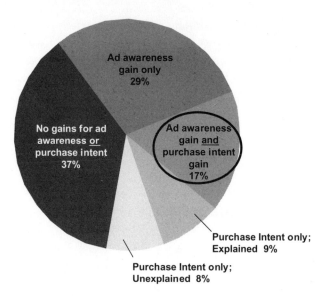

**Fig. 1.2** Recall + Persuasion of TV Advertising
*Source:* Ipsos-ASI Ad*Graph database.

databases that argue that the majority of advertising is working effectively. I am not suggesting that advertising does not work. There are plenty of sources to prove it does. The problem is that much advertising does not work well, and it is hard to be constantly successful at it. In turn, coupled with the previously discussed brand challenges, it is hard to build and maintain healthy brands.

Figure 1.2 comes from the databases of Ad*Graph tracking studies from Ipsos. The Ad*Graph tool is a standard set of questions within Ipsos consumer surveys, used to track the effectiveness of advertising. By using the same module of questions in each ad tracking survey, Ipsos has built a large database of thousands of objectively tracked campaigns. We track and review the consumer research on a week-to-week continuous basis, in-market, as the ad campaigns launch, build, and endure. To this consumer data, we include the media exposure levels (on air and off air) to assess how the media plan combines with the advertising creative to affect consumers and their brand perceptions (and behavior). We analyze the advertising breakthrough (the ad being recalled) by target consumers, as well as the consumers' desire to buy the brand. With all of this in-market survey data, the research consultant goes to work relating the advertising effects on the brand. In an overall analysis, across the database, we see that many campaigns fail to break through and get the consumers' attention, and half of those that do achieve breakthrough fail to motivate consumers in a meaningful away. Thus, only a small portion of campaigns work well (one in five). I appreciate that many ad campaigns may be designed to maintain high brand perceptions and not to increase brand motivation, but this objective is also often hard to achieve.

## MARKETING RESEARCH IS DIFFICULT

To add to the complexities of brand management, you can add the difficulty of marketing research. It is difficult for market researchers to accurately reach and elicit true answers from consumers. There is reluctance and a difficulty on the part of respondents to tell us how they truly make brand decisions. This makes it harder for marketers to really understand how to make better marketing programs.

If you ask a consumer why he or she buys a particular brand, the respondent is most likely to talk about rational features and rational benefits of the product or service. The respondent provides conscious, cognitive responses that are likely guarded, socially acceptable, and safe. Respondents will shy away from discussing true personal (potentially embarrassing) reasons for brand use. The respondent will also likely use cognitive thinking to provide expected answers to try to help the researcher.

What the respondents will likely not do so well is describe their personal driving motivations, their emotions associated with the brand context, their unconscious feelings, their personal values, and their aspirations. Often, respondents are not aware of all their emotions and struggle to describe them voluntarily. Additionally, some emotions are personal and perhaps embarrassing to admit aloud. Respondents might not care to mention all of their feelings, since some of these emotions may not be directly related to brand characteristics (but which can indirectly affect brand choice). We have also noticed that many respondents do not know how to answer when we ask them to tell us why they bought one brand instead of another.

As a case in point, consider a magazine advertisement we tested for a brand of chewing gum. We showed a sample of Americans a print ad for a

| | % |
|---|---|
| **Turned-on/attraction/sexy** | **21** |
| Trust/confidence | 8 |
| Content/satisfied | 7 |
| Excited | 6 |
| Fresh/refreshed/clean (breath) | 8 |
| Desire/motivated/inspired | 4 |
| Calm/relaxed | 3 |
| Extroverted/outgoing | 3 |
| Pleasure/pleased/happy | 2 |
| Easygoing | 2 |
| Disappointed | 2 |
| Hot | 2 |
| Cool | 2 |
| Bored | 1 |
| Tired | 1 |
| Excluded/lonely | 1 |
| Spontaneous | 1 |
| Popular | 1 |
| Young/youthful | 1 |

**Fig. 1.3** Emotions, Thoughts, and Feelings a Brand User Would Feel Using This Gum
*Source:* Ipsos-ASI R&D data.

leading brand of chewing gum. This ad shows two good-looking models, one male and one female. They are both looking toward her right breast, and the headline reads, "We know what you are thinking. Here is what you should be chewing." This ad is not about rational product features (for intense taste, or for long-lasting flavor, or for dental benefits of chewing). So this must be designed to affect brand imagery and emotions. Thus we asked consumers to tell us what "thoughts, feelings, and associations they would have chewing this brand of gum." This is an open-ended question to allow respondents to share whatever feelings come to mind.

The ad is obviously geared to sex, and the two models have been chosen for their sexy good looks. This is hard to miss, and I am sure each of us would immediately form some thoughts or emotional reactions related to the attractiveness of the two models in the advertising ("How did she get into those pants? What brand of jeans is he wearing? Why is he sitting like that? I wonder what she is like in person?"). Many of our thoughts are personal and unsafe to share in public. Figure 1.3 indicates what consumers told us about their thoughts, feelings, and associations.

Just 21 percent mentioned sexy and turned on! Is this right? What is the other 79 percent thinking? I can imagine that many more people felt some sense of turn-on, sexiness, or at least thought something about the attractiveness of the models—but respondents didn't feel comfortable saying so. The issue here is likely a combination of not wanting to publicly state their personal thoughts, not knowing how to answer, not knowing what is expected by our survey, and the consumer not completely identifying each of the feelings and emotional reactions he or she is having. In short, consumers are not good at surrendering to us their honest internal, personal, thoughts and feelings. For marketing research, this makes it hard for testing and evaluating effective advertising efforts. This is no small issue, because as we will soon see, much of our behavioral motivation is influenced by our emotional evaluation of stimuli and by our own personal gimmes. Thus, often what we say and rationalize is a cover or disguise for our more important inner personal feelings, aspirations, self-perceptions, and motivators. How many Mercedes-Benz drivers will admit aloud that they bought the car, in part, because they wanted to feel important or because they wanted to be perceived as being successful?

In summary, the pressure is on. Marketing managers can't afford to sit back. Successful managers are eager to seize the appropriate learning to find a competitive advantage.

---

### CHAPTER 1 TAKE-AWAY:
### PROBLEMS IN (MARKETING) PARADISE

Brand management is under attack.

- Old and familiar brands are stagnating.

- Humans desensitize to familiar stimuli. This works against old, familiar brands.

---

- Copycat brands are entering most product categories. There is growing proliferation of choice, with less differentiation among products.

- Substitutability among leading brands allows consumers to switch among a set of brands.

- Many product categories are becoming commodities, void of unique, well-supported branded choices.

- Retailers (grocery stores, drug stores, department stores, Wal-Mart, Costco) are gaining power, which influences how leading branded products are priced and sold.

- Consumers are becoming disloyal in their lifestyles overall and in their shopping traits.

- Internet shopping is enabling consumers to find lower prices.

- Advertising media are fragmenting; consumers are zapping and zipping through television, bypassing commercials,and they are ignoring Internet banner ads.

- It is difficult to constantly achieve advertising success. Many campaigns fail.

- To add to the complexity of brand management, marketing research is difficult and struggles sometimes to find the true drivers of brand motivation.

Marketing managers can't afford to sit back. The successful managers will take the initiative in learning to find the competitive advantage.

# MARKETERS' RESPONSE

**WHAT IS THE ANSWER TO THESE MANY (GROWING) PROBLEMS? IN SIMPLE** terms, brand managers have two fundamental elements of their brands: the offer (what the brand does for the consumer), and the price (how much consumers have to pay). How companies decide to manage these components will affect the success of their brands.

## COMPETING ON PRICE?

In response to these challenges to brand management, many marketers are reducing advertising support for smaller brands and reducing their prices to Costco, Wal-Mart, and other large retailers (or they bundle-pack multiple units, which also works to reduce the price per unit).

This is not at all ideal. Competing on price allows and even encourages consumers to evaluate brand choices (solely) on the same one basic criterion: price. As price increasingly becomes the main attribute to decide upon, the lowest-cost product will win. When marketers favor price discounts, sales promotions, and coupons (over advertising), it trains consumers to look for and even wait for such deals.

Promotions and price reductions help to move the sales volume of a brand; econometric sales modeling of such initiatives often show the positive impact of promotions. This is because such price reductions cause immediate and measurable changes in sales. Compared to the slow, gradual build of advertising and brand equity, price reductions are easier to measure. It is easier to model the sales impact of programs that cause quick changes than to model slow-changing measures such as the importance of brand equity. In turn, econometric modeling of marketing programs can over-claim the benefit of short-term promotions and may underclaim the long-term benefits of building brand equity. Price discounting squeezes profit margins, for the sake of quick volume gains, which leaves little support for advertising and for brand equity building. In turn, this causes the brand to become a low-price or discount brand over time.

Competition based on price is not a unique, proprietary, nor a patent-protected characteristic. Focusing consumer decision making solely on price encourages competitors because it is a nonproprietary element. Instead, it is advantageous to have consumers want to buy the brand for unique and desirable elements other than a low price (even at a premium price). And if we can create this desire specifically for characteristics that the lower-price brands and private-label brands cannot match, then all the better.

There is plenty of proof about the economic benefit of supporting strong brand equity. Just look at the market capitalization of Coca-Cola and Procter & Gamble (maker of Crest, Pampers, Pantene, Olay, and many other high-quality leading brands). These companies are worth considerably more than the value of their factories and assets and worth more than similar product manufacturers for no-name products (for example, makers of no-name cola beverages). Why? Because the consumers' equity and regard for their brands leads to strong current sales and good potential for future sales. This is valuable in financial terms.

A further analysis of sales promotions and coupons shows how unprof-itable they can be. Most consumers who take advantage of promotions are either current loyal users who would have bought the product even without the promotion, or they are occasional infrequent brand users who only buy the brand when it is on sale or being promoted. Otherwise, these occasional users will buy some other brand on sale. Thus, for current loyal buyers, the manufacturer's promotion is a give-away of profit that otherwise would have been earned (Look! A coupon for my favorite brand). For the occasional brand buyer, the promotion creates a purchase at little or no profit because the promotion costs more per package than the profit earned by the purchase. Furthermore, such promotions rarely convert a price shopper into a frequent loyal user (to purchase the brand when it is not being discounted or promoted). In sum, promotions are expensive and usually unprofitable. In the long term, every dollar used in such unprofitable coupon activity is a lost dollar for better support of brand equity to create a real desire to want a brand.

The same disappointment is found in the airline and retail sectors with their loyalty programs. A study by McKinsey & Company, (Cigliano et al. 2000) found that the investment in loyalty programs offered by large retailers can cost up to $30 million to create and launch, and up to $10 million annually to continue. This would require, on average, about a 6 percent increase in sales for the retailers just to break even. This is unattainable for most retailers, particularly when competitors launch similar programs and effectively cancel out the opportunity to steal customers to fuel the necessary growth.

I do recognize that some promotions are useful to help introduce a new product, to help clear out old inventory, and as a defensive mechanism to load up consumers with brand purchases before a competitor launches a new competing brand. Each of these reasons should be understood for their benefits and costs. If frequently used, we should realize that consumers get trained to look for promotional activity from a brand and will resist purchasing the brand when at full price. It is more profitable to compete by offering a superior brand equity that creates a strong desire in consumers for the brand even when at full price.

Within the Ipsos database for our brand equity assessment tool, Equity*Builder, we see proof of what contributes to brand success. The better a brand can perform for uniqueness, for popularity, for quality, and on emotional elements, the more successful the brand will be. In short, creating unique desired properties for a brand makes the brand more competitive, and more profitable than just offering a low price. The key information to be learned will be shared in Part 2.

## INNOVATION IS ONE ANSWER

We have seen many brands successfully compete by refusing to cut prices, choosing instead to innovate and to offer premium-priced products.

Consider Tropicana orange juice. In the 1960s and 1970s (prior to Tropicana's success), orange juice brands in North America could afford to advertise (because of their positive gross profit margins). Then, as the brands got locked into price wars, and with numerous sales promotions each year, they lost their profit margins. Consequently, they cut back on advertising and relied on price discounts to move sales volume. In turn, consumers learned to wait for the price reductions and to stock up in bulk. As a result, the orange juice category started to become a commodity, with private-label (retailer) brands competing head to head with national brands. Then came along a premium-priced brand, Tropicana, with a high-quality not-from-concentrate product at a considerably higher price. The product was superior in taste and freshness. In just a few years, Tropicana achieved great sales success. The implication is that consumers will pay a premium price if they get value in return. This innovation in the orange juice market was a great success.

Consider Gillette, who, along with many similar competitors, was making twin-blade razors. It could have been caught in a price squeeze as copycat brands matched Gillette in similar product performance. Instead, Gillette innovated and introduced a unique three-blade razor, Mach 3, sold at a premium price to great success. In January 2006, Gillette then introduced Fusion, a five-blade shaver.

We have also seen premium battery brands (Duracell and Energizer) innovate with a battery tester to provide uniqueness and relevance versus the lower-priced brands. We have seen the boring old toothbrush market in North America successfully innovate, including noticeably more expensive electric spin brushes.

Procter & Gamble is one of the most successful manufacturers of fast-moving consumer-packaged goods. Recently, P&G has been moving ambitiously toward innovation with new unique products such as Febreze, Swiffer, Crest White Strips, Mr. Clean car cleaner, and so on. These are not low-cost brands. They are successful because they are innovative, with good product performance.

Thus, one clear solution for manufacturers to support brand management is to innovate. This offers consumers new and unique reasons to buy a brand rather than a low price. Constant innovation makes it hard for the low-cost copycats to match the national leading brands. The lower-priced brands are not so innovative, and they need time to imitate the leading brands. Thus, if the leaders can keep evolving, they are harder to catch.

Innovation is not restricted just to the product itself. Brand owners may also innovate by changing how or where they sell their brands to consumers. If retailers such as Wal-Mart are squeezing the profits of traditional brands, then perhaps manufacturers can discover other ways to directly sell to their consumers (such as vending machines, kiosks, the Internet, and home delivery).

Additionally, innovation may include cobranding and partnering with other manufacturers or brands. Innovation may also include line extensions and evolving the meaning of the brand away from any one specific product category and more to an attitude. Nike and Virgin are two brands that come to mind. Nike was originally a running shoe brand, but today the brand stands for an attitude ("Just do it") with its name found on all sorts of sports and athletic products. The Nike brand is now less dependent just on running shoes. Another example is Virgin—originally a music store, but today the brand represents a free-spirited attitude permeating its music stores, airlines, and cell phones (among other businesses). This concept of evolving and innovating a brand toward an attitude and away from a specific tangible category or feature leads to my next major point.

## EMOTIONAL BRAND APPEAL IS ANOTHER ANSWER

Independent of, or in addition to, innovation there is also an opportunity to make brands more competitive by building emotional rewards for buying them. This is about creating emotional benefits beyond the basic functional requirements of the brand category. This may come in one of several forms. Some of the proven approaches (as seen in our Ipsos databases) include appealing to consumers' emotional associations; enriching brands with extra forms of sensory appeal; and creating marketing properties, characters, spokesperson, and icons.

For emotional associations, consider as examples MP3 music players and retail coffee shops. The focus of Apple's iPod campaign is on the appeal of imagery and personal emotion. Their silhouette creative campaign does not focus on rational product characteristics. In the portable music player category there appear to be other equally good, or even better, MP3 players, based on features and options. Instead, the iPod dominates its category by selling a cool, personal, emotional image.

Starbucks coffee also provides emotional payoffs well beyond the functional, rational concept of a cup of coffee. Starbucks is expensive compared to McDonalds, Dunkin Donuts, and many other large coffee retail outlets, yet Starbucks is enjoying great success by offering elements other then just the physical basic elements of coffee. There is the appeal of the friendly personal service, the appealing environment within the shop, the self-perception associations of holding a Starbucks cup in public, their appreciation of the environment, the perception that the coffee was made just for you, and so on.

In a unique internal R&D study conducted at Ipsos, we asked consumers to rate many different brands for whether they associated a distinct feeling, atmosphere, attitude, or emotion with each assessed brand and, if yes, to then let us know if they felt negative, neutral, or positive toward the association. Our goal was to see how emotional associations might influence perceptions of a brand beyond the raw basic purpose or requirements of the category. We found that the more a brand has extra appealing emotional associations, the greater the purchase commitment to the brand (see Figure 2.1).

As we will review later in the book, humans make decisions based on emotions, and they make decisions based largely on the expectation of positive rewards for themselves. The more a brand can add emotional rewards, beyond the physical rational performance of the product, then the greater the opportunity to be more competitive. Our Ipsos database proves this (reviewed later). Interestingly, this also applies to one person trying to persuade, encourage, or influence others: if we give emotional rewards to others, we are more likely to be liked and accepted. In turn, we can be more influential.

In the marketing world, using emotions to sell brands is easier said than done. It is not just a case of making emotional advertising. Marketers have to build emotional associations onto the brand, and these associations have to be personally relevant for consumers. These emotions must answer one or more of the consumer's gimmes. To be clear, good marketing is about selling brands via what consumers want to experience (what they want to

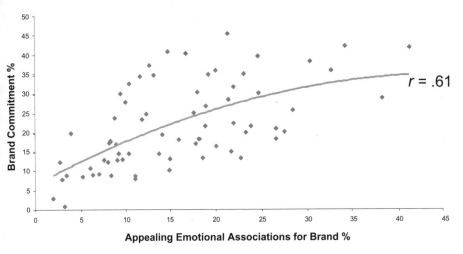

**Fig. 2.1** Brand Commitment by Appealing Emotional Associations. Each dot represents a brand.
*Source:* Ipsos-ASI R&D data.

hear) rather than by what manufacturers or advertisers want to say. Creating emotional payoffs of brands is definitely an extra way to stay ahead of low-priced brands, which can't easily afford to advertise or to build such emotional, personal associations.

Our senses are key building blocks for our mental activity, and they help to build emotional associations, memories, and attitudes. In turn, these bias our motivations. A tangible way to enhance the emotional appeal of a branded product or service is to create unique brand senses. At Ipsos, we often refer to this as the brand physique. Does a brand have any unique associations across the various senses? A unique touch or texture? A distinctive look (shape, color, and/or package design, such as the green tear-shaped Perrier bottle, or the blue Viagra pill)? A proprietary sound (like the sound associated with starting Windows on a PC)? A unique smell (for example, Johnson & Johnson's Baby Powder)? or a distinct taste or flavor (Listerine Original)? Some brands are now working to create unique sensory experiences and then legally protecting them as trademarks. Stimulating more of our senses is a useful thing. It is something that low-priced store brands are less apt to develop (so far).

Another way to enhance a product is through the creation of advertising properties, brand characters, spokespersons, or icons (such as Michael Jordan for Air Jordan shoes, Tiger Woods for Nike, Tony the Tiger for Kellogg's, The

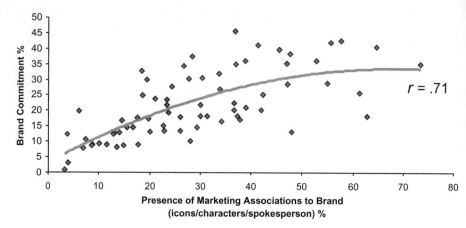

**Fig. 2.2** Brand Commitment by Marketing Associations. Each dot represents a brand.
*Source:* Ipsos-ASI R&D data.

Michelin Man, the Aflac duck, Ronald McDonald, and so on), or building extra marketing associations with other elements (such as the pink ribbon for breast cancer research, or Visa sponsorship of a sporting event), or both. These types of elements add an extra dimension beyond the functional product performance and enrich the brand with more elements to attract the consumer. We see this in our Ipsos data (see Figure 2.2). We observe that consumers have a greater attraction to brands that have extra marketing associations. It works.

I like to think of creating emotional personal associations for brands, and leveraging many unique senses, all as a part of emoti-suasion (emotional persuasion) This is the concept of persuading people by appealing to their emotional desires and needs: what does this brand give me? What emotional payoffs will I experience? Emoti-suasion is the core of all personal decision making. Enhancing a brand with many rich, appealing senses helps to give more emotional payoffs to consumers (more than a generic no-name product fulfills). This is the brand *give* for humans' gimmes.

## BE AWARE OF OVERENGINEERING

Another thing I find attractive about offering emotional brand-give is that you cannot really overdo it. You can do it badly, but giving emotional rewards to people rarely has a downside for a brand. I mention this because there is a downside or a limitation to relying just on innovation to stay ahead of low-price brands and copycat products. You can overengineer a brand, requiring a high cost and leaving an opportunity open for a competitor to offer a good enough product at a more competitive price. We will review the lesson learned about the concept of good enough later in this book (Part 2), but suffice it to say at this point that one can overengineer and overprice a brand, and copycat products can always, with time, catch up and match the innovation. Constant innovation, without other benefits such as emoti-suasion, is hard to achieve and harder to leverage in the long term. Constant innovation gets harder or increasingly removed from the core purpose of the product category or both. One has to be careful not to overengineer. Eventually, a brand will hit the limit of meaningful innovation. Is Gillette getting closer to overengineering their shaving product now that they have introduced their battery-powered, five-blade shaver, Fusion, at a premium price?

## A CALL FOR MORE SCIENTISTS IN MARKETING

To really leverage emoti-suasion (persuading consumers by leveraging emotional payoffs), we need to appreciate how humans tick. This book will try to expose the basics; however, I also think that many of our current marketing organizations are lacking the right skills. By marketing organizations, I mean all of brand management, plus advertising agencies and market research suppliers. As a whole, we are not knowledgeable enough about the various aspects of emotions, behavioral psychology, emotional needs, self-perception theory, genetic evolution, and so on.

In the early 1980s, when I was hired into the market research department at Procter & Gamble, in Canada, I was one of the few with a business degree instead of a degree in psychology, sociology, biology, or anthropology. Up until then, market research was mostly filled with graduates of such disciplines, but then things changed. The 1980s seems to have been a big era for MBAs and business school graduates. The problem is that people with business degrees, backgrounds in economics, or concentrations in mathematics sometimes lack enough sensitivity to the human sciences. I wonder if we need to return our focus onto the human sciences so as to understand behavioral motivations better. Most marketers today are ignorant of how consumers' brains work and how to best leverage their genetic wiring.

It is just lip service to believe that this is about making emotional advertising and offering nice, soft, irrational marketing imagery to consumers. There is much more to consider and appreciate. Emotional persuasion (emoti-suasion) is not just about creating an emotional response to advertising or for a brand. We see this in the Ipsos data. Just because an ad is emotionally charged does not mean these emotions are transferred to the brand in a meaningful way that will drive sales. We must learn more about triggering motivation into behavior and an actual sale. My exploration of emoti-suasion, for the writing of this book, has been mind-expanding exercise for me and far more complex than I initially appreciated. I am happy to share what I have learned and to share the proof found in the Ipsos databases of consumer research. This book is inspired by this whole opportunity to build emoti-suasion (the art and science of persuading through emotional association, senses, and emotional drivers).

---

### CHAPTER 2 TAKE-AWAY: MARKETERS' RESPONSE

Marketers need to respond correctly to protect profits.

- In response to the many challenges facing successful brand management, some companies are cutting prices, cutting marketing support, relying on promotions, and are playing the economic battle along with the lower-price brands.

- Promotional activity is rarely profitable. Competing on price is not a unique proprietary benefit for a brand. Any company can aim to compete on price.

- The likely winners of economic or price battles will be the retailers who control pricing, merchandising, and the preference for their own private-label products.

- Two appealing opportunities open for brand management are to innovate, with new unique, relevant product features or uses, and/or to add emotional rewards for using brands, beyond the basic functional requirements of the product (emotional brand-give). One can add these extra emotional rewards by selling or appealing to consumers' emotional desires, enriching a brand with more sensory appeal, and creating marketing properties, characters, spokespersons, icons, and so on. I refer to all of this as *emoti-suasion* (persuasion by appealing to human emotions).

- With innovation, companies needed to be careful not to over-engineer and overprice. Over time, innovation gets harder and may hit limitations. Copycat brands will eventually match whatever innovations you can achieve.

- You can do a poor job at emoti-suasion (appealing to emotional self-interest), but it is hard to overdo it. You can add emotional associations with communication and by enriching brands to appeal to the human senses. Some of these sensual characteristics can be trademark protected.

- The marketing industry is not likely well staffed with knowledgeable scientists who understand how humans are motivated (genetically). To leverage emoti-suasion, we need to go well beyond making emotional advertising. Marketers need to appreciate the human sciences.

# The Consequences of Our Genetic Evolution

*I have called the principle, by which each slight variation,*
*if useful, is preserved by the term Natural Selection.*
—Charles Darwin, *The Origin of Species* (1859)

**TO START OUR INSIGHTS INTO EMOTI-SUASION IT IS USEFUL TO START AT** the beginning and at the basic core of our composition as humans. Who we are and how we are made explains much about what we do.

## WHAT IS EVOLUTION?

Most readers likely know that genetic evolution refers to the biological changes that occur in a species, over time, from generation to generation. These changes are found in the DNA and genes of the organisms as the genes mutate, die off, or recombine in new unique ways. These altered genes give rise to new features or new characteristics in the organism (for example, a longer neck in a giraffe) and are passed on to future generations through reproduction. If these random mutations give an advantage to the organism population (a longer neck allows the animal to reach food better than others), then this can enhance the survival and reproductive advantage of the population. This ensures the future existence of the beneficial genes and their unique features. The species that evolve will live on in their new forms; the death of many species is caused by a failure to adapt to their changing environment.

Conversely, useless mutations and their associated genes tend to die off, since their presence does not offer an advantage. For example, many experts believe our ancestors might have had a tail, and since this did not help the survival of our species, mutants who had shorter (or no) tails were not disadvantaged. It might have been an advantage not to have to grow a tail and not to have the tail become a problem in some way.

The advantages of good mutations and the disappearance of useless ones are concepts referred to as survival of the fittest and natural selection. There is nothing conscious or intentional about natural selection. A species cannot wish something to grow or evolve (like wheels on our feet). Sometimes the impact of genetic mutation is negative, such as mutations of viruses leading to SARS and Asian bird flu. The point is that all organisms' genes are randomly mutating and changing, by accident.

Evolution is a unifying force for many of the medical sciences that are related to human beings. Evolution explains who we are, and, as best we know it today, explains why. As Theodosius Dodzhansky wrote: "Nothing in biology makes sense except in the light of evolution."

Proving a scientific theory can be impossible, but proving it wrong can be easy. In the light of DNA testing, fossil discoveries, and all of the past 150 years of scientific study since Darwin's *The Origin of Species,* nothing has proven the theory of evolution wrong. It has stood the test of time.

It was in Charles Darwin's work that I had hoped to discover explanations of human evolution, but Darwin spoke little about how his theories applied to mankind. His discussions often centered on birds, and he stayed well away from discussion of the human species (I suppose that in the late 1800s it was Darwin's preferred option—to stay clear of contentious social and religious beliefs).

Really, how different are homo sapiens from many mammals? Why shouldn't the theory of evolution and natural selection apply to us as well as it does for animals? We share many common features with birds, and we share common ancestors with apes and monkeys. Scientists use white mice for medical research because 85 percent of their genes and of our own genes are identical.

In his 1994 book *The Moral Animal,* Robert Wright has done a wonderful job advancing this topic. Wright discusses the work of key scientists in the 1960s and 1970s (over 100 years after Darwinism) whose insights extend Darwin's work of evolutionary biology into the social behavior of humans. Since the mid 1970s, new scholars continue to advance the theories of Darwin as they apply to humans. Robert Wright writes:

> Since the mid-1970s, the human angle has gotten much clearer. A small but growing group of scholars has taken what Wilson called 'the new synthesis' and carried it into the social sciences with the aim of overhauling them. These scholars have applied the new, improved Darwinian theory to the human species, and then tested their applications with freshly gathered data—slowly but unmistakably, a new worldview is emerging.
>
> The more closely Darwinian anthropologists look at the world's peoples, the more they are struck by the dense and intricate web of human nature by which all are bound. And the more they see how the web was woven.

Wright continues to describe how, in all cultures around the world, we share common recurring traits, such as the desire for social approval, common family structures, friendships, a need for social gossip, a sense of justice (an eye for an eye), feelings of guilt, and so on. Since our human composition ultimately boils down to our DNA and genes, then it stands to reason that commonalities of all humans rest in our genes. The social behaviors that hold our societies together must have a genetic basis.

Admittedly, there are cultural differences in our behaviors. In some cultures, grown males are not supposed to cry in public, while in other regions it is perfectly accepted (and even expected of men to cry when sad). Similarly, in some cultures people are not supposed to laugh without suppressing and covering their mouths (so as not to show the insides of their mouth) while in others, a good social laugh is made without such restrictions. Nonetheless, all humans tend to cry when saddened and laugh when amused. We all have these common genetic elements. Our unique (cultural) environments simply add degrees of difference to the exact manifestations of these genetic characteristics.

In our life span, the theory of evolution has been extended, with growing acceptance to humans. It is not that Darwin did not believe or intend his theory to apply to mankind—he simply avoided the controversies associated with doing so.

## INTELLIGENT DESIGN AND THE ANTI-DARWIN SCHOOL

Many people believe that humans (as well as animals) are the outcome of intelligent design: humans and animals are too complex to be the outcome of random mutations and survival of the fittest. The more religious believers in North America claim God is this intelligent designer and is the creator of Man.

As with any theory in favor of or against a concept such as the nature of the origin of man, it is impossible to prove a theory correct, but it is possible to prove a theory wrong by finding contradictions to it. To date, this has not happened to the theory of natural selection or to the theory of intelligent design. So we have a stalemate. Neither Darwinians nor anti-Darwinians are going to prove their theory right (or prove the other wrong).

Many smart thinkers suggest that the two points of view (evolution and intelligent design) need not be opposite views. It is possible and acceptable to believe in both. God could have made life in any fashion or manner, and he could have allowed natural evolutionary changes to be part of his master plan. God could have designed life with the intention for it to evolve. That is, evolution is part of God's plan.

Recent documented history shows that animals are changing due to the environment (diet, medicine, weather, impact of mankind), due to interbreeding of pets, the cross-mating of wild animals, and so on. Animal species are being created while others are going extinct. Things are evolving, but the question is what role God plays in this. God could easily have planned for natural law and evolution as part of his intelligent design. To date, the Vatican does not reject the theory of evolution: the Catholic Church describes this evolution as God's master plan for how things were to develop. There is no proof for or against any answer. Thus, the debate about the history of mankind is a question of belief.

The growing evidence in support of evolution (regardless of whether evolution is by design or by random deviations of genes) begs us to consider its implications for explaining our behavior.

## WE ARE THE PRODUCT OF OUR GENES

In our present state, humans (with our many strengths and weaknesses) are the outcome of tens of thousands of generations, with slight randomly occurring genetic mutations, which have given us survival advantages. Our organs and our features are a consequence of this evolution. Since our brain is also an organ, it, too, is a consequence of evolution (with all the aspects the brain entails, such as memory, emotions, sensual stimulation, subconscious processing, etc.).

All around the world, humans feel love, guilt, selflessness, selfishness, grief, altruism, social needs, and so on. These are feelings we are all aware of, but why do all humans have these elements? In short, there is a genetic explanation, found in evolutionary science. We are composed of genes, and therein lies the answer. We all have a love gene, a grief gene, an altruistic gene, and so forth. To learn more about the explanation for each of these human characteristics, I suggest Wright's book *The Moral Animal*. Just one small example from his book provides a case in point about the influence of our genes.

> The evidence so far is that grief does comply exquisitely with Darwinian ex-
> pectations. In a 1989 Canadian study, adults were asked to imagine death of
> children of various ages and estimate which deaths would create the greatest
> sense of loss in a parent. The results, plotted on a graph, show grief growing just
> before adolescence and then beginning to drop. When this curve was compared
> with a curve showing changes in reproductive potential over the life cycle, the
> correlation was strong. But much stronger—nearly perfect—was the correlation
> between grief curve of these modern Canadians and the reproductive-potential
> curve of a hunter-gatherer people, the Kung of Africa. In other words, the pat-
> tern of changing grief was almost exactly what a Darwinian would predict,
> given demographic realities in the ancestral environment.

The study of such genetic evolution allows us to explain everyday life better, to appreciate how we act, to explain choices we make, to clarify goals we have, and to explain our moral composition. We can use this learning to better understand how we make decisions, how we are motivated, how advertising works, and how motivation leads to behavior. If there is an evolutionary explanation about why we are wired a certain way, then doesn't it make sense to take advantage and leverage this?

## HUMANS HAVE HABITS

An interesting phenomenon among humans all around the world (and for animals as well) is the occurrence of habits. We all have habits, and they affect our behavior. Why do we have habits? There must be an evolutionary advantage; otherwise, habits would likely have devolved as unnecessary genetic baggage.

We all know the concept of a habit. It is the tendency to follow a regular or consistent (repeated) practice. Over time, habits can be conducted automatically or subconsciously, with little thought. In evolutionary terms, this is the benefit of habits to the animal kingdom. By having habits, (1) we do not have to engage the brain (which takes energy), and (2) we can avoid risks and dangers by sticking to the safe, proven path (literally).

In the wild, among the trees of a forest, or the wide open plains of prairie grasses, we can find animal paths. The habitual practices of animals walking the same paths, repeatedly, have worn into the vegetation and dirt. Does it matter which side of each tree a deer walks by? Not likely. A forest is full of randomly scattered trees, and each square meter is quite similar to the one next to it, but animals habitually walk the same paths day after day. Why? In short, there is a survival benefit. The benefit is that the deer do not have to think or worry about their path because when they last walked it they were not hurt or killed. Nothing bad happened; thus, all things being equal, it is better to follow the same path next time. Additionally, having habitual practices allows us to conserve brain energy. We do not have to rethink every time when the same situation presents itself. The brain only has to recognize and remember that the path was safe. It's a no-brainer.

Consumers have habits and follow similar (automatic) routines each day. Have you ever noticed we tend to sit in the same places at the dining room table, in conferences or meeting rooms, and did so in university lecture halls?

Forming habits is closely related to learning. That is, (1) some stimulus is present, (2) we try it, (3) if the consequences are pleasing, we repeat it, and (4) by repeating it, we develop a place for it in our brain that is easily (and almost automatically) triggered. We are comfortable with the familiar, and we do not like change or conflict.

The implication of habits is important to the marketing world, as consumers tend to have purchase habits. For consumers, many of their brand decisions (in favor of one product over another) were made a while back, perhaps years ago, for some product categories. Since then, consumers habitually follow the same brand choices without much thought because it is a risk-averse practice. Admittedly, for some categories we might have a couple of brands in our preferred set. Nonetheless, we tend to have made our decisions a while ago, and often fall into a habitual purchase pattern. Yes, we might expand or evolve over time to include other choices in our preferred set, but our tendency is not to change.

Good habits are appreciated, especially in the marketing and sales world if consumers are habitually buying your brand. What if consumers do not have the desired habit? What if they habitually buy the competitive service or brand? What if your child habitually does something that is not right? Such habits need to be altered, and this acts against our genetic wiring.

Imagine not having a memory and thus having no habitual practices. Every purchase decision would have to be rethought and reevaluated, which would be a waste of time and energy. Consider the simple task of buying a brand of deodorant or antiperspirant. When our current brand runs out (or in advance of the empty deodorant container), many of us intend to repurchase the same brand without much thought. This is a quick and easy decision. We do not have to think why we like this choice versus all the other possibilities. We just habitually repurchase. Now, imagine if we did not have this habitual practice, but instead we had to stop to decide which product to buy each time. There are so many forms, varieties, scents, sizes, and prices to choose from. We may make a wrong decision and be disappointed, and it would take time to review the packages and decide. Grocery shopping would take hours if we did not have our habitual purchases. Habitual programming is so strong in humans that we might not even be perfectly happy with our current brand, but we may still habitually repurchase it to avoid engaging the brain and risking a worse alternate choice. We are programmed to disengage the brain and follow familiar paths; this is the problem if the consumer is habitually not buying your brand.

Habits are based on a genetic disposition, so it isn't easy to break them (consider people who habitually bite their nails—it is hard to stop that habit). To help the sales effort and to motivate a brand's nonuser toward a trial purchase, we can't be subtle. We need to abruptly intercept and interrupt the consumer's habitual purchase process. We must get the attention of the consumer to force his or her brain to engage and consider the alternative. Like the deer in the forest, we need to block the path with a fallen tree before he or she will consider a different path. Consumers tend to prefer the familiar and then desensitize to it (autopilot mode). Just like the saying when dealing with bad choices: better the devil you know than the devil you don't. How many people with house or car insurance habitually renew their annual policy without making even the tiniest effort to find a better deal? How many people are constantly switching brands of underarm antiperspirant to find the best choice—and keep evaluating new ones when they are introduced into the marketplace? Not many. This is not what humans like to do.

It gets worse. Not only do we need to disrupt undesirable habits, we then have to trigger or activate the desired attitudes within the consumer, assuming they are already there. For example, we might know or believe right at this moment that it would be a good idea to get competitive quotes the next time we need to renew our auto insurance, but unless we have the right trigger at the right relevant time, the attitude does not get acted upon. This leads into the concepts of attitudes, of triggering them, and of motivation, which will all be discussed later.

Gerald Zaltman, author of *How Customers Think,* talks about humans having memories so that we can forget. I think what he means by this is that once we have evaluated our decision criteria and settled on a choice, we then only have to remember that we like the choice. By only remembering that we like the brand, we no longer need to remember all the details about why we like it. In my mind, this is similar and related to having habits. Remembering so we can forget and having habits both allow our lazy brain to avoid thinking, and once the brain locks in on a decision, it becomes a challenge to get consumers to change.

So to summarize, habits are genetically established, and in evolutionary terms, they are beneficial. In order to break them, we need a disruptive engaging stimulus that is strong enough to invite brain activity to consider an alternate decision (brand choice). This is the challenge to marketers. Being subtle and mainstream is not likely to work so well.

I saw a quote on a calendar that made me laugh because of how well it applies to us all: "Insanity is doing the same thing the same way and expecting a different result."

## DETECTING IRREGULARITIES

Another genetic trait of humans and animals is the capacity to detect irregularities in our world. Why is that? Why are we good at detecting the odd one out? The obvious answer is that there must be a survival and reproductive genetic benefit.

Detecting irregularities appears to be an outcome of hunting and gathering food. For example, when lions hunt, they approach a herd of prey and look for the weakest, easiest kill. This is for their own survival, because each hunt is dangerous to a lion (a hoof kick from their prey to the head can be fatal). Thus, the lions that could best detect the weakest prey likely lived longer, and in turn, passed on this ability to detect the weak prey to their offspring. For humans, we had the same incentive to detect irregularities. Imagine picking berries in the wild. Some look ripe and healthy, many are average, and some might have bugs in them or be rotten. There is a survival benefit to be able to find the ripest ones and to avoid the diseased or infected fruit. An inability to detect the best and worst food likely led to sickness or even premature death. So for millions of years of living in the wild, our species, like the lion and other animals, has been rewarded for detecting irregularities.

Today, our ability to detect irregularities is a reminder of our genetic history—but by no means has this trait disappeared. Just go to a market where they sell fresh produce and watch shoppers pick and choose. We are still rewarded by our ability to detect the ripe items and avoid the spoiled ones. Admittedly, the risks and dangers are less obvious in our abnormally safe and contrived environments, which we have created for ourselves in just the past millennium. Nonetheless, we still choose as if it mattered to our survival.

Over ninety-eight percent of man's existence was based on our hunting-and-gathering behavior. Detecting irregularities has become well established in our genes and will not disappear quickly.

For marketing, and for many other things in life, if we want to get attention and be recognized, we have to be irregular (stand out from the crowd). Such irregularity appeals to consumers' genetic disposition to give attention and to evaluate it. This is likely not so newsworthy, but the opposite is likely what is important. By being boring and regular, items blend in and are not well detected. If you couple the concept of desensitization with the concept of irregularity, we can see that there is a real need to avoid the status quo if you want to get consumers' attention. It is key to have constantly new, unique (irregular) stimuli to engage the consumer brain. Brands should not stand still, nor should their advertising.

## NOT TOO MANY FACTS

Genetics again, and our physical brain. When it comes to making decisions, it appears humans do not like (or do well) dealing with too many choices. Perhaps having many choices is a consequence of our modern history, and we have not evolved quickly enough. For millions of years, our brains developed slowly as a consequence of the environment at the time. Life was simpler for our brains. Our original ancestors were not faced with so many decisions as a typical consumer faces today in most regions of the world. In the beginning, decisions were simpler: fight or flight. Do I pick this berry or that one? Do I hunt the baby or the big healthy parent?

Today, more than ever, we have so many choices as to what to wear, what to watch on TV, which one brand to buy within each category, where to travel in the world, and so on. Frankly, our brains have not genetically evolved well enough to efficiently deal with the volume of such complex decisions. The brain did not gain genetic benefits for being able to deal with complex decisions, so it has not evolved in that direction. The escalation in the number of choices we now face has happened too quickly for humans to have evolved and adapted. For the longest time, we did not have to deal with such complexities. It is as if our brain counts: "one, two, three, a lot."

When faced with many choices, humans tend to isolate and focus on just a few key criteria and ignore more than they can comfortably deal with. When faced with many different criteria to choose or assess, we often arrive at a feeling of "I can't decide what to do." I don't know about you, but I prefer a restaurant menu with a smaller selection of items (or wine list) than the multipage menus. There is too much choice. How can I possibly decide? As a consequence of too much choice, humans chop the list of choices, classify things into generalized groups, or reduce the criteria to a smaller, more manageable set.

A popular study illustrates the challenge of choice. This was conducted in a neighborhood supermarket in California, in 2000, by two professors, Dr. Sheena Iyengar (Columbia University) and Dr. Mark Lepper (Stanford University). Dr. Iyengar writes about this in her web site link at www.columbia.edu. Consumers in the store encountered either a display featuring 6 different flavored jams or a display featuring 24 different jams. All consumers who stopped by the displays were offered a $1.00 off coupon for the purchase of any one of the jams in the displays.

The larger display, with 24 different kinds of jams, attracted 60 percent of the passersby, while the smaller display attracted only 40 percent. What was quite surprising was that only 3 percent of the consumers who visited the larger display (and received the $1.00 off coupon) made a purchase. This compares to the 30 percent purchase rate from the consumers at the smaller display of just six jams. This is a tenfold difference in favor of the display with less choice. This appears to support the theory that humans are not well equipped to deal with too much choice and will experience negative feelings (anxiety) that lead to inaction.

For marketing and sales, the consequence is to manage the decision set for consumers. In everyday life, we should also offer just a few choices to our children and friends, whether for dinner, for some activity, for a choice of movies to see, and so on. It does not serve us well to oversupply choices, as it is not well received by our brains.

## COGNITIVE DISSONANCE: CONFLICTING BELIEFS

*Cognitive dissonance* is another genetic trait of our evolution, found among people around the world. This is the concept of having opposite attitudes, or experiencing conflicting thoughts, toward something. This could be conflict between beliefs, values, emotions, desires, and so on. These conflicts, or dissonance, often lead to an unsettling or negative set of feelings. Humans do not like cognitive dissonance. We act to reduce or eliminate the conflicts, often changing or downplaying our beliefs or searching for other beliefs to tip our feelings in favor of one direction.

The theory is that humans strive to have a consistent set of beliefs so that our thinking is nice, neat, and comfortable. In evolutionary terms, we appear better served to have a comfortable and easy time of dealing with our beliefs so that we can make future decisions in an anxiety-free manner. It is better to avoid too many conflicting beliefs, so as to avoid uncertainty, doubt, and complexity. Conflicts would make it harder to form a quick future decision (which could be life threatening). It is better to always have a clear, settled set of beliefs (to be prepared).

I experienced cognitive dissonance the other day while flying overseas to France. I chose to fly in business class with Air France rather than Air Canada. I felt that the French food, wines, and hospitality would be better.

I was personally disappointed and found the experience to be less than I expected. Business class is expensive, and I expected good service. So I started to rationalize that at least the seats in business class are better than in economy, and this is what is most important for sleeping in the overnight flight. Thus, I started to discount the importance of the food, wines, and videos, and added greater importance on getting a better sleep in business class, even though sleeping is not the fun part of being in business class. I altered my values to justify the price I had paid, and I have now altered my beliefs about the rewards of business class (no more cognitive dissonance).

When purchasing goods and services, cognitive dissonance can be a common feeling. After a purchase, we may find another product or service with a lower price or with better features. This may be somewhat upsetting. So we try to postrationalize why our first purchase was a good one to help reduce the anxiety. Retailers and marketers can likely do things to reduce cognitive dissonance. Companies can consider follow-up communications to reinforce a consumer's good decisions, to allow the person to vent or discharge his or her frustration, and to help make good on a disappointment (I know of two different airlines that have offered departure gifts at the end of the flight for those in business class. Perhaps this helped to correct any dissonance). We will cover the role attitudes play and how they affect behavior later. Attitudes are important, and so is our genetic evolutionary trait to eliminate feelings of cogitative dissonance.

Cognitive dissonance is just another example of how we are all wired alike and how such an understanding can allow marketers to be better sellers. These various characteristics, such as habits, detecting irregularities, cognitive dissonance, and so on, are common in all humans. They are just a few examples about learning how humans are wired. By understanding such characteristics marketers, and all of us in general, can learn how to be more influential in dealing with family, friends, and consumers. The characteristics described here are quite basic, simple elements. Many more powerful human characteristics exist that influence our motivations—namely emotions, cognitive decision making, our subconscious, our senses, short-term versus long-term memory, and so on. Chapter 4 starts our review of how these elements work.

To end this chapter about genetic evolution, I would like to share a bumper sticker I saw the other day. It gave me a smile: Celibacy is not hereditary.

## CHAPTER 3 TAKE-AWAY: THE CONSEQUENCES OF OUR GENETIC EVOLUTION

To understand how to sell on emotions we have to understand how humans are wired.

• Humans are the result of genetic evolution, and we share common characteristics, as a species, all over the world. These features are found in our DNA and genes.

• Intelligent design is not inconsistent with genetic evolution, because it may be a part of the designer's (or designers') master plan.

• Nothing has proven the theory of evolution wrong in the 150 years since Darwin wrote about it.

• If we are wired a certain way, it is useful to learn how to best leverage our evolutionary traits.
  —Humans have habits, and we are wired to follow them.
  —We are wired to detect irregularities and notice things that stick out from the norm.
  —We are not good at dealing with too many facts or complicated decisions.
  —We oppose inconsistencies or mental conflicts and will work to find an acceptable solution, whether it is smart, right, or rational.

• These traits are basic. Many more powerful human characteristics can be incorporated so as to increase our ability to influence and motivate others. These include emotions, cognitive decision making, our subconscious, the role of our senses, short-term versus long-term memory, and so on.

# CHAPTER 4

# MECHANICS OF THE BRAIN

**THE HUMAN BRAIN HAS MORE NEURONS THAN ALL THE STARS IN OUR** galaxy. This is quite a concept to contemplate, and it alludes to a complex organ, but it need not be intimidating or a reason not to understand the basics of how the brain works. They say the most important four inches in the world is the distance between our ears, so I think it is useful to make an effort to learn more—it helps explain how advertising works!

In my opinion, it is not important to understand in detail the biological or chemical functioning of the brain in order to learn how to motivate humans. We can skip the details, but I have come to appreciate that a little insight into how the brain works helps to explain how an emotion is formed, how memory happens, how we make decisions, why we have habits, and so on. So let's cover the important elements.

My interest in neuroscience took a leap forward in 2004, prior to some necessary back surgery on the lowest part of my spine. I had two herniated discs that needed attention, and my family doctor advised me that the best kind of surgeon to seek would be a neurosurgeon. This surprised me, because I did not appreciate that neurosurgeons would occupy themselves with the lower spine. I thought that neurosurgeons were mostly, if not exclusively, interested in the brain.

The reality is that the brain sits on top of the whole nervous system (nerves, spinal cord, and brain), which receives the many messages from the external world (the appearance of a great-looking piece of chocolate layer cake, an exotic-smelling perfume, the touch of an extremely soft piece of cloth). These senses pass through the nervous system into the brain. In turn, the brain deals with them, evaluates them, assesses if they are good or bad, initiates a response if anything should be done, and stores the sensory experience.

Within the brain, there are different characteristics or parts. The flow of information is processed in different places with different functions. The basis of it all is neurons.

## NEURONS: THE BITS AND BYTES OF THE BRAIN

Neurons are the millions and millions of brain cells that biomechanically make it possible for the brain to work. These are like the little bits in a computer that are either on or off (sending a signal of zero or one), and each neuron has dendrites, or tentacles (sometimes many hundreds of little branches *per neuron cell!*), that touch up with those of other neurons' dendrites (see Figure 4.1).

Information passes along or through these cells via miniature chemical reactions in each cell, similar to how electricity passes through the millions of bits in a computer, turning them on or off. The combination or pattern of the many bits being on or off represents a unit of information—a byte. Similarly, in our brain, the pattern of neurons firing represents a unit of information. A specific pattern of firing neurons is called an *engram.*

There are approximately one hundred billion neurons in the adult brain, and each neuron connects with approximately ten thousand other neurons. This yields about one thousand trillion connections. In total, this creates a lot of possible permutations and combinations of how neural patterns (engrams) can fire. There is no shortage of possible neural patterns to process or to store engrams! And interestingly, we have so many connections in our brain that, after childhood, it is believed the number of circuits in our brain

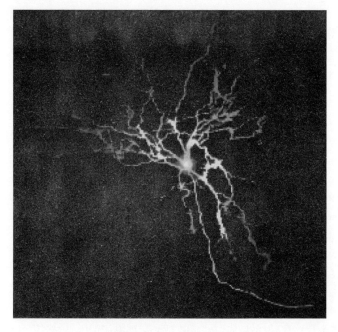

**Fig. 4.1** Brain Neuron

reduces to clean out the unused and unnecessary ones. In turn, this makes more room for the remaining ones to be more powerful and efficient.

Over time, as adults, it also appears that if we do not use and stimulate our brain by constantly learning and engaging the brain, then more neurons and neural connections decline. It is believed that Alzheimer's and Parkinson's diseases lead to cells dying, which results in a loss of connections between neurons—hence the loss of mental powers. There can also be chemical imbalances in the brain that disrupt normal neural firing activity. Many psychiatric illnesses are felt to be due to such chemical problems, which reduce the normal operations of the neurons. Menopause is also believed to have a similar association with chemical balance within the brain, which can lead to the alteration of various senses, functions, emotional control, and judgment.

Although many illnesses cannot be avoided by wishing as much, adults can perhaps help themselves by constantly using, engaging, and challenging their brains. Brain activity helps to encourage neuron growth and to maintain the many connections in the brain. Use it or lose it. When one stops using one's brain—upon retirement, for example—the brain may get less of a workout and start to lose its power.

## MEMORY: A PATTERN OF FIRING NEURONS

Unlike a computer bit, our brains are not magnetic, and the cells do not stay on or off electrically. Once a neuron receives an electrical signal, reacts chemically, and sends off its signal to its neighboring neurons, the cell then returns to neutral until another signal comes to it. So how then does the brain store signals as memories?

Since there are millions of neurons leading to trillions of connections, there exists a massive network of possible paths for brain messages to follow. As each unique stimulus or signal flows into the brain—for example, the smell of a freshly baked apple pie—multitudes of neurons start firing. The unique interaction between each neuron sets a pattern. The first time this happens, the signal gets the specific neurons to fire in a new fresh pattern. Each involved neuron affects the others in a minute chemical way such that the next time a smell similar to that of apple pie enters the brain, it follows the same path (the same neurons and synapses) as previously established. A similar but different smell (say, the smell of burnt toast) would follow a different pattern of neurons and synapses, and the next time you smelled burnt toast it would more or less follow the previous pattern of neurons and synapses for burnt toast. These patterns of neurons, their chemical electric changes, and their linkage with other neurons set the patterns that are the basis of a stored memory.

Since our memories are built on these patterns of how various neurons fired, the strength of this memory will be affected by how strongly or how many times this signal comes into the brain and this neuronal pattern fires. One can already see how advertising and marketing can be important in how memory is burned into the brain. The nature of the message and the repetition of the message will affect the burning-in of the neuronal pattern.

Cells live and die, they can be damaged, and our brains can be chemically altered. These neuronal patterns, once created as a memory unit, may break down, leading to a loss of the memory. Thus, over time, we seem to be either adding to our memories (via repetition and use of the neuronal patterns), or we are weakening memories (by disease, injury, or a lack of use of the brain).

## FUNCTIONAL AREAS OF THE BRAIN

I recall the first class of Psychology 101 I attended at university; the professor entered the lecture hall and declared that war has been good to psychologists. Quite a shocking statement as a means of introducing yourself to new students! But we have learned a lot about the brain from accidents and war victims. A hundred years ago, war injuries were a leading source of insights into how the brain worked. There is the story of a man named Phineas Cage, who lived in New Hampshire in the 1850s. One day, an explosion in the mine where Phineas worked shot an iron rod through his skull and through his brain. It did not kill him: he survived and recovered—partially. The iron rod damaged the front part of Phineas' brain, and in turn, he lost his sense of emotions. Apparently, Phineas' intelligence quota (IQ) was not altered from this accident because intelligence rests in a different part of the brain than was damaged by the iron rod. From examples like this and the history of other brain injuries, scientist have learned that damage to the back of the head affects vision, damage to the side of the head affects speech, and damage to the front affects decision making.

When I was a young boy, I was dyslexic. Dyslexia causes difficulties in learning how to read, spell, and write. I could correctly do math, but I would then write down the numbers backward (for example, 7 plus 7 would be written as 41). Dyslexia is theorized to be biological in origin, and even a genetic issue, but it can be overcome. Due to my initial learning problems, I visited a medical clinic for testing. One exercise required me to view a picture with one eye, then close it, open the other eye, and draw the same picture. Another test required me to wear headphones: in one earpiece, I could hear a stream of letters, and in the other earpiece, I heard a stream of numbers. The doctor asked me to repeat what I was hearing so as to determine which ear was stronger and how this was linked to my communication. I had several other similar tests. The idea behind these tests was to explore how well the two sides of the brain were working and how the different centers of the brain were communicating (visual to muscle coordination, audio to speech, visual to languages, and so on). Fortunately, dyslexia can be overcome with much work—this book is evidence of that!

The stories of my dyslexia and Phineas Cage's accident show that brain activity is based on neurons firing to each other and that there are patterns—different centers of the brain for varying functions. For our memories, these neural patterns are not stored in any one part of the brain, but instead are spread throughout the brain mass. There are centers of the brain that deal with different types of messages.

By using the latest medical technologies for scanning brains, such as magnetic resonance imagining (MRIs), doctors can observe the activity of the brain as it processes various different stimuli, such as the taste of a drink compared with looking at a picture. An MRI image is a vast improvement over X-ray images because it does not expose the body to dangerous radiation and it offers much greater detail of soft tissues. As the name implies, the MRI machine uses magnetic fields (and computers) to detect the different densities of materials (relying on the properties of excited hydrogen nuclei in water in our body). This is harmless to patients (unless they have any metal in their bodies, which would be strongly affected by the magnetic fields). MRIs can be used for viewing inside the brain, detecting between the different densities of the brain matter, and detecting changes due to blood flow and brain activity. A functional MRI, or fMRI, registers changes in brain signals due to changing brain (neuronal) activity.

We all likely know that the brain is more or less spherical and that it has two halves, the left brain and the right brain. There is also an outer part of the brain and an inner part. The outer part has the appearance of a walnut, wrinkled and folded with ridges as if it was stuffed into our skulls. This outer part is the cerebral cortex, and compared to all other mammals, the cortex is a large part of the human brain. Many experts believe it developed later in our evolution than the inner brain. Some say that the cerebral cortex grew so quickly relative to the growth of our skulls that the cortex is literally crammed into the skull (not important to our purpose here perhaps, but curious). This cerebral cortex is believed to deal with issues of language, reading, writing, judgment, abstract thought, creativity, and other characteristics that can be easily thought of as human characteristics (and not so well established in animals that have much smaller cerebral cortices).

In between the two halves of the brain, joining the cerebral cortex of the left with that of the right, is the corpus callosum. This works to join the different functional activities and centers of the brain—like a network cable. One side of the brain is usually responsible (more active) for a particular skill or function (e.g., for vision), while the other half of the brain excels in other functions (e.g., speech). It is important to link these functional centers for the operation of the entire body. For the majority of us, speech is on the left side of our brain, while vision is on the right. So when we see something and want to describe it to a friend, our right side (for vision) needs to communicate with the left side (for speech) via the corpus callosum.

## Split Brains

Due to an illness, accident, birth defect, or other cause, the corpus callosum joining the two hemispheres of the brain sometimes does not work properly. As a result, the different functional centers of the brain do not network together well. A person suffering from this condition may see and recognize a horse (as processed in one area of the right brain), but this signal does not network well with the center of speech on the left side of the brain, and thus they cannot state what the object is.

## Déjà vu

Déjà vu translates from the French as "already seen." This is the feeling we sometimes get when we experience something and we feel we have already experienced this before, but have not. A popular explanation for déjà vu is that there is a miniscule delay in time in information being shared from one half of the brain to the other. That is, one area of the brain gets the original or initial signal, and milliseconds later it gets to the other side of the brain that is most responsible for that function (be it vision, speech, or taste). In turn, we have a fleeting feeling of having already experienced it.

## Synaesthesia

Our eyes detect light, turn this into neuronal signals, and send them to the brain. Our nose obviously does not process light signals, but instead it detects chemical smells and sends these separate signals to the brain. For those who suffer from synaesthesia, the signals from the senses are mixed up, such that the processing of one sense is confused with that of another. For example, a smell may trigger perceptions of color, or certain colors trigger perceptions of smell, or a confusion exists between any combination of the five senses. In a manner, these people can smell color, taste a feeling, or see music. Scientists aren't sure what is happening internally, but they feel that it is some form of cross-wiring or mixup with neuronal patterns, as one sense is causing neuronal firings for other senses.

Inside the cerebral cortex is our old brain, which many experts believe was the first part of the brain to have developed as we evolved. It's often described as the "lizard brain," because it developed (many million years ago) before the cerebral cortex. It is not hard to appreciate then that the function of this initial lizard brain relates mostly to basic animalistic issues, such as evaluations of our environment to assess danger and to offer a quick response of fight or flight, to control hormones, to look after muscle coordination, and so on.

Inside and under this inner brain, we get to the real core of the brain and brain stem. Here we find the parts of the brain that control our heart, blood pressure, body temperature, respiration, and organ function.

In a nutshell, the main difference between our brain and that of other animals is the development of the cerebral cortex. This is where the intellect and abstract thinking of humans comes from. Within this large outer area of our brain, we have several lobes and functional centers (see Figure 4.2).

## THE GROWING BRAIN

It is believed that the brain is not at all fully developed when a newborn emerges. It is not fully wired, and it is still building more neurons and connections after birth. Many experts suggest that mothers give birth at nine months so as to get the newborn out of the womb before its head gets any bigger. After birth, the brain continues to develop. Recent scientific studies indicate that the last part of the brain to finish developing is the front of the cerebral cortex, which does not finish developing until after the teenage years. Thus, it is no coincidence that many (smart) teenagers make poor decisions. They do what mature adults think of as stupid things ("what were you thinking?" we scream), but the frontal lobe, which is the home of emotions, judgment, and decision making, is not yet fully developed. So teenagers are prone to poor judgment: they are *not* biologically mature

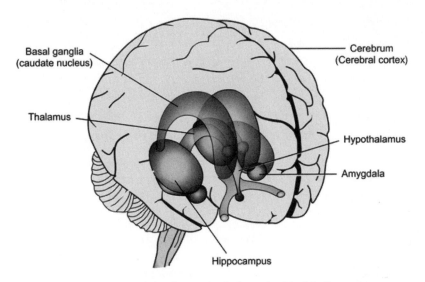

Basal ganglia
(caudate nucleus)

Cerebrum
(Cerebral cortex)

Thalamus

Hypothalamus

Amygdala

Hippocampus

**Fig. 4.2** Parts of the Brain, Including the Limbic System

enough to make their own decisions, as their emotional judgment centers are not yet fully developed. Parents can now cite science as a legitimate reason to help guide their teenager's decision making!

## EMOTIONS IN THE BRAIN

An important area of learning is concerned with emotions. Emotions are a mental state created from reactions to our senses. Because emotions are not the messages themselves, but instead are a reaction to the stimuli, an MRI does not easily observe emotions. We know we have emotions, and we know that certain types of brain damage cause a distortion or loss of emotional processing (damage to the front of the brain). Thus, we know the brain has a specific way of dealing with emotions, within the frontal lobes of the brain.

The front of our heads is extremely vulnerable to damage due to auto accidents. In turn, doctors have observed many effects of damage to the frontal lobes, such as reduced facial expression, loss of potentially strong social behavior, loss of judgment, reduced language skills, loss of decision making, and poor problem solving. Many of these elements relate to our ability (or inability) to determine what is right or good versus wrong or bad.

Because of this, experts consider these elements to be emotionally affected and consider the frontal lobe as the home of emotions.

The role of emotions is so critical to us that it justifies a whole chapter dedicated to it (later), but before a review of emotions, it is worthwhile discussing our five senses. These are the raw functional building blocks of our nervous system and our brain activity, and it is with these senses and sensual signals entering our brain that emotions come into play.

## CHAPTER 4 TAKE-AWAY: THE MECHANICS OF THE BRAIN

- Neurons are the cells of the brain that act like interlinked bits in a computer. As a stimulus enters the nervous system and is transmitted to the brain, it fires a unique pattern of neurons. Each stimulus fires its own unique neuronal pattern, and this forms a unit of memory (an engram).

- The brain has different functional areas. These can be seen with the use of MRI machines, which use magnetic fields and computers to look into our brains, without radiation damage or pain. MRI machines allow experts to see activity in different parts of the brain and other soft tissue.

- The brain does not fully mature until well after birth. The last portions to develop, in the late teenage years, are the frontal lobes of the cerebral cortex. This is where emotions are stored. This slow development helps explain why teenagers often make poor decisions or judgments.

- Emotions are felt to be mostly stored in the front of the cerebral cortex. Damage to this part of the brain affects emotional processing. In turn, the ability to make decisions is reduced because one can't evaluate positives versus negatives. Thus, emotions and decision making are linked.

# CHAPTER 5

# PROCESSING OUR SENSES

**ALTHOUGH WE KNOW OTHERWISE, WE HAVE BEEN DISCUSSING ALL** incoming stimuli as being similar, whether they come from our eyes, our nose, or our fingertips. But not all stimuli entering our nervous system are equal; the quality and nature of stimuli from the five senses differ. We detect our environment with different capacities across our five senses, and our brain allocates different amounts of space to each.

The main role of our five senses is to allow us to monitor our environment and to react in ways conducive to survival and to reproduction. Some of our senses help us better than others, and the development of our senses has been different from that of other mammals (for example, compared to other mammals, humans have a good capacity for vision, but a quite poor capacity for smelling). The bundle of sensory capabilities humans possess today has evolved to suit our particular existence (so far). Our species tends to rely on our brainpower to offset our comparative disadvantages of smell and hearing.

Although our nose may be complex, our ability to smell does not compare to that of a dog, nor does the percentage of our brain dedicated to smell match theirs. More than two-thirds of a dog's brain is dedicated to its sense of smell. I had the opportunity to visit the dog-training center at the Canadian customs department in Rigaud, Quebec, where government border guards train dogs to detect drugs and explosives. The trainer I met with described how sensitive a dog's nose could be. He told me that a dog could smell each unique vegetable in a beef stew, whereas you and I may only be able to smell the overall effect of the stew. Apparently, dogs can smell fear in humans as well. Border guards are also teaching dogs to smell large amounts of currencies by the smell of the paper and ink on the cash.

We also know that taste is largely influenced by smell. How many of us as children held our noses when we had to eat something that tasted bad? We tend to lose our ability to taste when our nose is blocked. Taste is not just affected by our nose, but also by our eyes (the appearance of the food). Our brain has learned that certain colors and appearance represent certain taste profiles. If one altered the color profile of orange flavored Jell-O by making it purple, or changed the appearance of a glass of white wine by adding a few drops of red food coloring, we can trick the tongue and brain into accessing other taste associations in our head. Our eyes will alter the taste experience.

For humans, vision is relatively important. Our brain dedicates a fair amount of capacity (neurons) to our vision, more than to our nose or ears. When we interact and communicate with someone else, we may use words, but over three-quarters of our communication is nonverbal. That is, we may hear the words, but we are also using our eyes to detect body language and facial expressions, whether we make eye contact or not, and we pick up cues from the speed of the words, the emotion and tonality of the speech, and so on.

We also quickly judge people we first meet in about two seconds of visual contact. Yes, we may alter our opinions afterward and we may add further evaluations to our initial visual assessment, but we are quick to judge our environment and elements in it based on what we see.

In his book *How Customers Think,* Gerald Zaltman reviews how humans think in terms of pictures, associations, and icons, and not in text or words. For example, if you were to say "elephant" to someone, they are likely to arrive at a vision of a big grey animal with a trunk, to consider a circus or Africa, or to think about Dumbo (and so on). That is, we are more likely to have associations than we are to visualize the letters E-L-E-P-H-A-N-T. This power of vision has implications for advertising and for communicating with people. Marketing and advertising, in particular, need to leverage visual elements and to show the message. We will cover this later.

## THE ENTRY OF A SENSE

Every stimulation of each sense flows into the brain and is processed. It is (nearly) impossible to turn off the body's ability to detect and process sensual stimuli. So what happens with the constant bombardment of sights, sounds, touch or feeling, smells, and tastes?

As a stimulus enters the nervous system and flows to the brain, it initially passes through the limbic system (the basic initial lizard brain). This quickly assesses if there is any danger and any need to take corrective action—much more quickly than the cerebral cortex. Scary, fearful, dangerous stimuli are immediately processed by the amygdala, just at the point of entry into the brain, a part of the limbic system in the lizard brain. Dangerous signals immediately fire into the hypothalamus, triggering muscle activity and even an adrenalin rush. This is instinctive and has been this way since the days of our earliest ancestors. In a way, the limbic system has become so efficient because it has been around the longest. This automatic and immediate processing makes us jump or flinch when we are startled. The fear response fires without having to be thought about in the cerebral cortex. The cerebral cortex would slow us down, using up precious time to react to real danger. Meanwhile, the signal coming into the limbic system *also* gets attention from the cerebral cortex in deciding or thinking what to do. This is a slower part of the brain, and it is where we run through many possible decisions and reactions. Thus, once startled by our limbic system, our "thinking brain" may then tell us to calm down, because it has had a chance to deduce that the signal or stimulus does not represent danger. Conversely, if there is real danger, our "thinking brain" leads us to take the right corrective action. For example, if I am in a safe, quiet neighborhood in the middle of the afternoon, and I suddenly hear a loud bang, I might initially flinch, with a moment of fear. But then my cerebral cortex thinks, assessing if the sound was familiar and determining the best thing to do. Perhaps it was a gunshot and I need to duck for safety. On the other hand, perhaps it was the backfire of a car engine. In this case, I decide to do nothing. In extreme cases of fear, the amygdala in our inner lizard brain may overpower the cerebral cortex and nervous system, leading to stress, shock, and paralysis.

What about nice stimuli? Pleasurable stimuli do not get much attention in the amygdala and pass right into the cerebral cortex for further processing. One key area in the cerebral cortex is what experts refer to as the *reward center*. This is the part of the brain that seems to light up when pleasant stimuli are being felt. It is also associated with the release of dopamine, which causes a pleasant feeling in the body. Drug rehab experts often refer to this part of the brain when discussing the addictive nature of drugs and alcohol consumption.

• • •

To tie this all together, we can summarize these mental building blocks:

1. All stimuli entering the body are processed in the limbic system, and an emotional judgment (association) is made. That is, each set of neuronal firings is tagged and scored emotionally as bad or good. Each emotional association is tied to that memory unit and added to our experience. This process is the result of genetic survival and allows us to exist in our world.

2. We cannot stop stimuli from entering our brain. Everything creates an emotional response, not just emotionally nice things. Every entering stimulus is evaluated and tagged.

3. The more stimuli associated with an event (or brand), then an increased mental activity and emotional tagging is going to happen. In turn, this builds more emotional associations with the event and fires in more ways into the cerebral cortex. We will see later why this is important.

4. Many emotional associations are subconscious. Although our brains are constantly processing stimuli and emotional associations, we are not always aware and thinking about them. Our conscious brain engages when necessary and when we need to think about something.

5. These stimuli, along with their tagged emotional evaluations, become the basis for how we decide what to do. These are the building blocks and drivers of our motivations.

## DESENSITIZING TO STIMULI

Have you ever noticed that when you detect a smell in a room that, over time, you adjust and lose your sensitivity to the smell? Do you feel your watch on your wrist right now, or a pierced earring, your underwear, or the ring on a finger? Probably not. Why is that? Your body initially detected each stimulus (the first odor when you entered a room, or the feel of your underwear when you first put it on), and it reacted. This is a natural process and can't be stopped. The initial stimulus was processed in the limbic system and emotionally evaluated and tagged based on previous neuronal firings for these same stimuli (from the previous day, for example). After your brain has assessed and judged the stimuli, it no longer wastes energy continually concentrating on it. Your watch is still on your wrist, but the body no longer pays much attention to it. This is a natural energy-saving process for the brain. It also helps to avoid sensory overload in your head.

A useful insight about desensitization applies when eating. As we take a bite or a drink of a beverage, our taste buds react to the sweetness, acidity, saltiness, and bitterness to form a taste profile. If we take another identical taste of the same food or beverage, and then a third, the brain will start to desensitize to this stimulus because it has already just processed and judged it and is now getting back to a neutral state to prepare the mouth to be ready for the next new (possibly threatening) stimulus. Thus, your brain is literally beginning to lose the taste detection for this food or beverage, but when you introduce another different food item or beverage, the tongue and brain will jump into action to evaluate this new stimulus. A fresh stimulus triggers an engagement of the brain. So the consequence for eating is to alter every different mouthful of your dinner. You will taste and enjoy each bite a little bit more. This is why wine tasters will often rinse their mouth with water or bite into an unflavored cracker or white bread to cleanse and neutralize the palate prior to tasting a different wine. The water and cracker prevent a desensitization building up from constantly sipping wine after wine after wine. Try alternating every mouthful at your next dinner and enjoy the heightened taste experience from each different bite.

The implications of desensitization are large to the advertising world: Our brains gear down on the continuous presence of familiar old stimuli. Thus, old familiar advertising that keeps being aired gets tuned out as we become familiar with it. Brands that are much the same in look and presentation, year after year, get little attention from us. Again, our brains have made their evaluation and no longer pay so much precious attention to the familiar known things. On the other hand, our brains are programmed to detect, process, evaluate, and emotionally tag *new* stimuli. For new stimuli, we pay attention and judge it for threat or pleasure, and we build new neuronal networks. Thus, new advertising, new packaging, and new ways to think about a brand catch our attention.

## SENSORY DEPRIVATION

It appears that our senses are so important to the functioning of our brain that prolonged isolation or deprivation of external sensory stimulation can result in depression, anxiety, and even hallucinations. A little, short-term deprivation of (some) senses may be relaxing, but several studies imply that humans need sensory stimulation to function properly or happily. A Dutch experiment in 1992 was designed to explore the effects of sensory deprivation on voluntary prisoners. Volunteers were locked up for 24 hours in prison cells especially designed to cut out sound, light, and any contact with guards. Half of the participants were unable to make it for 24 hours. It appears that humans need to be able to influence their own situation and have some forms of control over their own life.

In *Science Matters*, Canadian David Suzuki writes about how modern humans living in urban industrialized centers spend 90 percent of their time indoors in environmentally controlled environments. These environments deprive us of the rhythms of the outdoor world (which influenced our genetic evolution for thousands of generations), the air is cleansed, the lighting is constant, sounds are disguised with white noise, and textures are commercial and uniform. We are starving our senses of their natural balance, and this may be adversely affecting our mental and physical health.

In everyday life, a temporary lack of sensory stimulation means the brain is less active. In turn, one may get sleepy, leading to a quick doze. Imagine a long car drive, a long boring university class, or sitting down in front of the television. Once the environment becomes familiar and consistent, the brain may start to shut down, with sleep coming soon after. This can lead to embarrassment or even danger if one is driving a car. A quick trick is to eat or put something in the mouth (a mint, a piece of candy, a bite of an apple). This stimulates the taste buds and the sense of touch in the mouth. In turn, this stimulates the brain into action and puts off sleep (for the time being).

Thus, our senses are not only important for us to detect our environment, but they are also necessary to our well-being. We crave the stimulation of our senses. They enrich our world—and they can enrich brands.

## BRAND SENSATIONS

Personal motivation and behavior can be affected by our senses. We can't stop our body from processing senses as they enter our nervous system, so perhaps creating extra sensual associations with brands can be effective. To explore the concept of human senses, the emotions they trigger, and resulting human behavior, Ipsos initiated research with consumers about the association of senses with brands and the effects senses might have. I had already heard on television that casinos in Las Vegas have been experimenting with different scents in their casinos. They have found that different scents injected into gambling rooms affects the levels of gambling from their visitors. Some retailers have also discovered that different music broadcasted in their stores can affect shopping behaviors.

In our study, we asked respondents to assess a few different brands within a specific category. We covered 15 different categories, covering 75 everyday products such as bar soaps, toothpastes, stomach remedies, colas, batteries, food wraps, shoes, and so on. For each brand, we asked respondents to rate it on the five senses: Does the brand have a distinct smell or scent? Look? Sound? Feel or texture? Taste? For each that had a distinctive sensation, we then asked respondents to tell us how appealing the sensation was (positive, neutral, or negative). As you can appreciate, some brands have quite a unique look, taste, or smell, but might not be appealing! We built a summary score across the five senses, which combined the presence of a distinct sensation, the appeal of this sensation, and added up the scores across all five senses. The higher the summary score the more sensually enriched the brand.

Theory would suggest that a brand rich with appealing sensations should fire more neurons across the brain, and thus have a better burn-in, with more emotional associations. In turn, this might lead to more positive

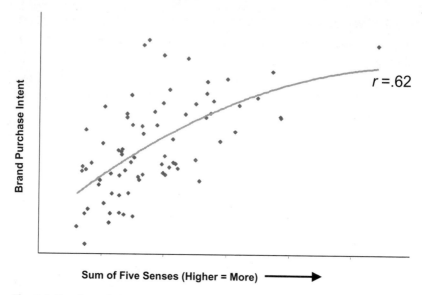

**Fig. 5.1** Purchase Interest versus Appealing Sense Associations. Each dot represents a brand.
*Source:* Ipsos-ASI R&D data.

interest in the brand. When we reviewed the 75 brands in our study, we found a positive correlation between brand purchase interest and the level of appealing sensations (see Figure 5.1).

The look of the brand has the strongest contribution to purchase interest, perhaps because we rely heavily on this sense or because the brands were more likely to have distinct appearances, shapes, or colors. Other than the look of brands, research on the everyday products we all use shows that many brands do not have distinct, appealing sensations. Figure 5.2 shows how each of the five senses is associated with a brand (the presence of a distinct sensation and the appeal of this sensation).

It would be tempting to conduct such sensual research on obviously distinct brands, but when we choose to focus on the mainstream everyday categories, we observe a large opportunity for brands to do a better job building distinct sensations. Not only can this make a brand stronger, but some of these distinct characteristics can also be patented or trademarked. In turn, this will offer protection from copycat products. The data supports the view that enriching a brand with distinct sensations is useful in building brand equity and competitiveness.

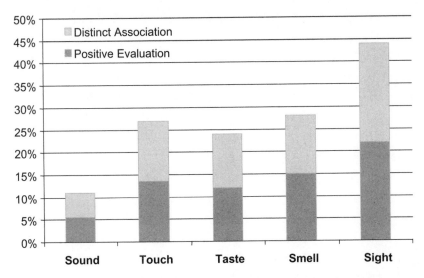

**Fig. 5.2** Association of Senses: Summary of Distinct Senses Averaged across 75 Brands/15 Categories

## CHAPTER 5 TAKE-AWAY: PROCESSING OUR SENSES

• The main role of our five senses is to allow us to monitor our environment and to react to it in ways conducive to survival and reproduction.

• Our brain activity is largely influenced by vision. We judge our environment and other people mostly through our eyes.

• As our senses detect a stimulus, it is transmitted to the limbic system of the brain and is quickly evaluated as either positive and appealing or dangerous and bad. Each incoming stimulus is tagged with an emotional association.

• We cannot stop stimuli from entering our brain, being evaluated, and getting an emotional association. Our brain is not actively selective. Many associations are built indirectly and subconsciously.

- To compensate for information overload, the brain desensitizes to familiar stimuli. The body starts to ignore familiar stimuli and readjusts to a neutral position to be able to detect new stimuli. Advertising and familiar brands are subject to such desensitization. One needs to keep providing various (different) new stimuli to avoid desensitization.

- Brands that are perceived as having several appealing distinct associations across the five human senses (a distinct look, texture or feel, scent, taste, sound) earn greater brand equity and purchase interest. Brands can increase their competitiveness by creating unique sensual characteristics, and these can possibly be trademark protected against copycat products.

# PUTTING MEMORY TO WORK

*"It is a poor sort of memory that only works
backwards,"* the Queen remarked.

—LEWIS CARROLL, *Through the Looking Glass* (1872)

**WE CAN'T STOP THE STIMULI FROM ENTERING, FIRING DIFFERENT NEURONS**, being evaluated, and being tagged with an emotional value. These engrams are created mostly unintentionally, passively, and subconsciously. Consider for a moment your childhood and the first few grades in elementary school. Can you picture the school? Your classroom? Your desk and table? Most of us can almost walk through a virtual vision of our first grade classroom in our head. Did you intend to remember this? Why do you still have this in your memory all these years later? What good is it going to do you today? Perhaps you also recall certain smells associated with your classroom (the smell of the janitor's cleaning fluids, or the glue from arts and crafts). All to say, we can't always control what gets into our brain and what is well engrained in our memory.

By the way, are you feeling any emotions, good or bad, as you recall the visions and smells associated with your first year in school? Are you sensing any emotions of childhood, anxiety or worry? Perhaps you are smiling right now as you recall these early memories. This is our brain at work, recording all types of received stimuli and emotionally tagging them. As we recall the memories, they come tagged with emotional associations.

Experts tell us these units of memory are burned into our neural networks by several characteristics:

- Duration of the stimuli and its neuronal processing

- The intensity or richness of it

- The relevance or importance of it

- The simplicity of it

- The quantity or repetition of firing this same engram (memory) over time

- The quality of the emotions attached to the memory

- The health of your cerebral cortex where the neuronal pattern resides (hopefully no disease or damage has happened)

These characteristics are where advertising and persuasion begin. It all starts with how beliefs, feelings, and attitudes get into the brain and are stored. Naturally, it also matters how the memory is retrieved later, but first things first.

We also know about short-term memory versus long-term memory. Short-term memory is the initial, quick holding pen that drops or forgets things in about two minutes (or less). In order to get past short-term memory into long-term memory, the item needs to match some of these previously listed elements. That is, the engram needs to have some level of importance or impact to be worthy of being well stored in our memory; the more intense or important, the better. Perhaps this is why we remember our early childhood school days; they were traumatic to us at that stage in our lives, hammered home each day as we were forced to leave the comfort of our mother's apron to experience this scary new world.

We reviewed in the previous chapter the value of senses and the capability of enriching a brand with many distinct sense associations. Part of the benefit of enriching the brand across several senses is that it helps to create a better neuronal burn-in for the brand into our long-term memory. The greater the number of senses involved, and the more emotionally appealing these associations are, the better the chance for getting into long-term memory.

## THINKING IN UNITS OF MEMORY

Any single incoming stimulus fires upon tens of thousands of neurons—if not more! This creates a lot of brain activity, neuronal firing, and complexity. In an effort to summarize these activities, and to catalog them well, it appears as if the brain summarizes each complicated firing as a unit. It is as if our brain is creating simple memory units (associations, visions, mnemonics, and metaphors) to simplify future retrieval of these neural engrams. Gerald Zaltman (author of *How Customers Think*) talks about memory being in units (metaphors, icons, etc.) and that we store things largely as pictures. In our complex environment, we simplify stimuli into units as a way to cope and deal with the huge overload of stimuli. By having simple units in our heads, it is easier to organize and retrieve them later. Units are easier to deal with than a mix of words and text without a unifying theme or story. This is the whole idea behind the concept of a mnemonic, which is a system or device to remember a bigger, more complex thing. Many of us like to use mnemonics as a simpler way to remember things. The unit helps us to store and retrieve details that are more complex. Here are some mnemonics that might be of interest.

- The Five Great Lakes in North America?
  *Mnemonic:* HOMES
  (Huron, Ontario, Michigan, Erie, Superior)

- The planets in our solar system?
  *Mnemonic:* "My very educated mother just served us nectarines"
  (Mercury, Venus, Earth, Mars, Jupiter, Saturn, Uranus, Neptune. Pluto has recently been reclassified!)

- The coordinates of the compass? (one of the first mnemonics my young daughter learned).
  *Mnemonic:* "Never Eat Shredded Wheat"
  (North, East, South, West)

- "I before E except after C." This one drives me nuts because I can't spell a word without this phrase ringing in my head.

- Order of the colors of a rainbow?
  *Mnemonic:* "Richard of York Gave Battle In Vain"
  (Red, Orange, Yellow, Green, Blue, Indigo, Violet)

Let's also try a little memory exercise about pictorial units of memory versus unrelated numbers. Here are two sets of numbers to remember. Don't write them down, but try to memorize them. We will then revisit them in a few pages. If you like, consider these as a message from an advertisement to you, the target:

7 0 4 1 7 7 6

6 1 2 1 7

Related to remembering things, humans appear to like stories and fables. In almost all cultures, we rely on stories to remember our history and to teach lessons. Almost all cultures use storytelling to pass on learning and memories. Why? Because they usually come enriched with quality emotional associations (the ability to visualize the story), they take a while to burn in (long "firing" period getting the story in), a simple story or fable is easier to capture as a single memory unit, and we can often find some relevance in them. Contrast this to memorizing historical dates, the names of all the U.S. Presidents, or memorizing the preceding numbers.

## ADVERTISING MEMORY

By now, we should all have an appreciation of how enriched memories burn into our brains and that our brain is lazy (energy efficient). The brain works well in pictorial units, stories, and mnemonics, and it likes discrete, consistent messages. It works well with simple Big Ideas. With this in mind, what do we find when we turn these insights to the advertising industry? Do we find proof that advertising works better when it leverages how our human brains work rather than ignoring or fighting against our wiring?

Ipsos has tested and tracked all types of advertising styles, approaches, creative ideas, content, and so on. We have various different standardized research tools, used all over the world, to pretest and evaluate new advertisements (Next*), and to measure the effectiveness of advertising once in-market (Ad*Graph and Brand*Graph). From these tools, across thousands of studies, we have established wonderful databases that allow us to review successful and unsuccessful advertising efforts.

We have learned that advertising that focuses on a unified storyline

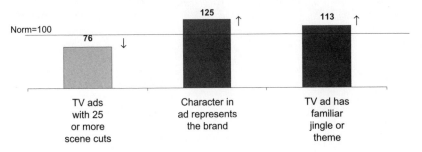

**Fig. 6.1** Related Ad Recall in Next*TV Database of Pretests

performs better than advertising that offers a cut-up, fragmented collection of video shots. Ads that use many fragmented scenes earn below-average unaided recall by consumers. (Being able to recall an advertisement is a key component of advertising success.) These multicut ads may be nice, pleasing, entertaining montages, but the brain struggles to file and later retrieve these types of ads (in general). They often lack one unified storyline to tie the images into one neat, easy-to-remember unit for our brain. On the other hand, using a brand jingle, an established iconic character, or a familiar brand theme helps to earn better recall of the advertising. Figure 5.3 shows the average level of ad recall for ads with these different characteristics. The normative score is 100 in our ad pretest research. Ads with lots of scene cuts tend to perform below norm, likely because they are so fragmented and make it difficult for our brains to easily file (see Figure 6.1).

Creating entertaining advertising or using humor are also good ways to earn recall. Such advertising excites and engages consumers. This aids the brain in terms of filing the memory in an enriched manner. Conversely, boring, irritating, or soft, emotional, or moody ads tend to underperform for recall. These ads fail to create positive neural activity in the cerebral cortex, and thus do not burn into long-term memory so well (see Figure 6.2).

Another problem for advertising memory (once ad recall is achieved) is correct brand attribution. In advertising, it is critical to tie in the brand name with the creative big idea of the ad. One of the most significant failures of advertising in our Ipsos tracking databases (in all regions) is poor brand link. Consumers can remember the ad but fail to recall the advertiser. Too many ads on TV are useless because they entertain but fail to get the correct brand identification across to consumers.

Previously we talked about the video montage style of ads. If these types

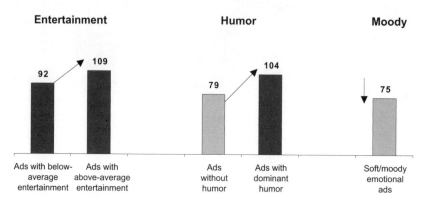

**Fig. 6.2** Related Ad Recall in Next*TV Pretests

of ads get on-air, we often find that along with weaker ad recall, consumers also struggle to correctly recall the advertised brand. Brand link problems are not just restricted to this multicut style of advertisement. We observe brand attribution problems across all styles of advertising. Even the ads that try to leverage the way our brains are wired by following a single storyline may fail to achieve good branded identification. This can happen because the storyline is not about the brand or fails to integrate the brand as the main focal point. Many ads can be 30 seconds of theater that have little to do with the brand.

In advertising, the brand should be *undeniably* linked to the simple creative idea of the ad so that when the little memory unit is burned in, the brand identification is burned in equally. This is more problematic than getting ad recognition in the first place. Why? Because ad stimuli often get into the brain, even if they are subconscious and unintentional. We also need to get the brand into the brain, linked with these ad ideas. When we ask consumers to recall an ad for a given brand, many are not able to do so, but if we then show them the actual on-air ad, a larger portion of people will tell us "Ah, geez, I've seen that ad." So for many people, the ad has got into their brain; however, if the memory unit is not linked to the brand, and if the brand name can't recall or trigger the ad, then this advertising is not as effective as it should be. The advertising equity must come to the consumer's mind in order for the ad to influence brand motivation to its fullest.

An interesting exception to the branding challenge is the minority of brands that use unique logos or brand icons within their advertising and on the packaging in the store. Some ads may fail to achieve correct brand name identification, but by using a proprietary icon, consumers can use the icon recognition as the method to find the brand. For example, there is a brand of laundry fabric softener in Canada called Snuggle that has used a talking teddy bear in its advertising. If the consumer cannot recall the brand name from the ad, it is still possible to link the ad message when shopping because the same distinct teddy bear is found on the Snuggle packaging. Although the brand name may not be registering, the visual branding property of the teddy bear aids visual memories.

From a memory filing function, there are three key elements to be achieved by advertising: (1) break through and get into our memory; (2) be properly filed in an enriched manner for easy recall; and (3) be correctly branded (or linked) to the advertiser. The first step is about avoiding the regular and being different enough to stick out. We have seen that humans are wired to notice the irregular and to desensitize to the familiar. For the latter two components, the advertising needs to successfully intertwine these two elements, along with the message, into one memory unit. This is the concept of building the Big Idea of the ad around the brand. The Big Idea is the simple, short, two-sentence description you would give to a friend who has not seen the ad. If the ad description is about the creativity and fails to include the brand as a central part of the story, there is a risk of the ad being filed in the brain without brand attribution. The memory unit lacks the unification of the brand. This failure makes it harder to achieve ad success.

This idea of branding and linking is much more involved than showing the brand logo or package shot. This applies to television ads as much as it does to magazine advertising, newspaper ads, billboards, and so on. The creative big idea that forms the basis of the unit of memory (the engaging part of the ad) must be undeniably associated with just the one brand. This can be trickier than it appears. I recall a Canadian television ad for toothpaste. It used close-up video shots of a series of the brand's packages falling over like a sequence of dominoes. As the packages fell against each other in a multiple sequence, the camera started to pull back to show the visual domino effect of the packages forming a smiling mouth, with white teeth. This took 30 seconds to reveal, with nice lighting and various camera angles. It was intriguing and captivating. The 30-second ad consisted of showing the brand, with thousands of packages, and yet the ad suffered a brand link problem. In our research, we observed good recall for this ad when we described the big idea to consumers (the falling packages like dominoes) forming a smiling mouth), but consumers struggled to remember which brand was being advertised. It seems most people liked seeing the artistry of the falling packages (like dominoes) to see the patterns, and timing sequence. This was the engaging part of the ad, as we watched to see what would be revealed, but the big idea was not undeniably linked to any one brand of toothpaste. It could have made equal sense for Crest, or Colgate, or Aqua-Fresh, or Close-Up. Perhaps if the brand name was "Dominoes" then the ad would have been undeniably linked, but this was not the case. The engaging creative idea failed to be linked to the brand despite showing viewers thousands of package shots.

## LOW ATTENTION PROCESSING OF ADVERTISING?

Some advertising specialists (namely, Robert Heath in the United Kingdom) argue that as long as an advertisement gets into the brain, it has the opportunity to help support the desired brand attitudes in a favorable manner. These people suggest that for an ad to be beneficial, we do not need to be consciously aware of the advertising, and we do not need to be able to recall the advertising ideas when asked about the particular brand name. They refer to this passive role as *low attention processing* (LAP).

An illustrative example may help. For example, we can ask consumers if they can recall any recent advertising for Colgate toothpaste. Some people will say yes and go on to accurately describe the right advertising for Colgate, but some consumers will say no—they cannot recall any specific recent advertising for Colgate. In our survey, we will continue by describing the recent Colgate advertising or showing it to respondents. A portion of respondents who initially could not recall any Colgate advertising will now recognize the actual ad that has been on air ("Oops, sorry, I have seen that ad recently!"). Overall, about 25 to 35 percent of consumers can recall seeing an ad when it is shown to them, but cannot recall it without help. The ad is in their head, but not consciously recalled. A major part of this problem is due to a lack of attribution to the correct brand. That is, these consumers remember the (entertaining) ad, but do not recall the brand name. Thus, when asked to recall the advertising for the specific brand, they cannot retrieve any correct ad memories. In a sense, this ad without brand linkage is acting as (unbranded) entertainment.

We find in our ad tracking databases that about 8 to 10 percent of consumers can have recall with correct brand attribution for advertising when helped with a description but who otherwise cannot voluntarily recall the advertising. That is, they have the ad in their head *and* they know which brand is being advertised, but they cannot recall the ad voluntarily. Robert Heath suggests that these people can still be affected by this vague ad recall. He refers to this phenomenon as "low attention" or "low involvement processing." Interestingly, we sometimes find in our Ipsos studies that this group with LAP can indeed have better brand attitudes. It is as if their subconscious memory has still allowed or caused the advertising to aid the brand equity. This LAP shows that the power of our brain is not restricted just to the conscious memories that we can identify and recognize. Our advertising memory can also work subconsciously. However, the percentage of respondents with this LAP is usually small, and it does not always lead to positive brand impact for the advertiser. The effects are neither as strong nor as useful as those among consumers with good conscious volunteered ad recall.

## ADVERTISING REPETITION?

Another memory consideration for advertisers is the concept of repetition. In advertising, we see this repetition by being exposed to the same advertisement over and over again on television, in magazines, or across many different billboards. Psychologists talk about repetition as a way to get an item into long-term memory. This may be true, up to a point, but it is not necessarily the most cost-efficient approach for advertisers. Repetition (often referred to as *frequency* in advertising) is costly in terms of media dollars. So what do we think about repetition for our advertising memories?

We all know about short-term memory. Practically all of us have experienced the frustrations of something going into our short-term memory that we then cannot remember 15 seconds later. Consider a new, unfamiliar phone number that someone leaves as a voice message. If we do not write down the number on paper, many of us would have to repeat the new phone number over and over again in our minds as we plan to return the call. Once we have dialed the phone number, five minutes later many of us will likely have forgotten it. The repetition of the number helps to keep the memory alive (in short-term memory), but it really does not get into long-term memory unless it is enriched with relevance, emotional qualities, seeing the number, or perhaps building mnemonic devices to remember it (such as recalling a historic date for some of the numbers). We know that repetition works, but only to a degree. *Instead, it is more cost effective for advertisers to get the memory embedded in their targets by relying on fewer ad exposures and leveraging other tools to achieve memory.* As discussed previously, we can achieve better memory by building quality inputs (involving multiple senses, making the ad relevant, focusing on one big idea as an easy metaphor, mnemonics, or icons, leveraging visuals, and so on). Relying on repetition is less effective and more costly. Remember, after we become familiar with a stimulus, we tend to desensitize to it.

From the many lessons learned within our advertising databases, I think the single most important one is that creative is king. What I mean by this is that the ad itself is important, and much more so than the number of times the ad is seen by consumers. In our database, we observe that after a constant amount of TV media exposure across thousands of ad campaigns (all at the same amount of cumulative media exposure), the amount of difference in ad recall, in brand identification, and in sales impact is wide. Since the media exposure is fairly constant, we are left explaining the wide variation in impact based on the nature of the ad itself. Some ads are great, and other ads are terrible. Spending lots of media money to get lots of repetitive media exposures for a terrible ad is not going to miraculously make the ad campaign a success. The concept of repetition and frequency of exposure is well down in the list of important factors for successful advertising. This has two big implications to advertisers:

1. Make sure your advertising stimulus is good for your target (before spending expensive media dollars). The way into long-term memory is better achieved through an enriched, relevant, emotional ad (versus repetition of a mediocre ad at great cost in media dollars).

2. Put your money into reaching your entire target before worrying about repetition.

After seeing an ad a couple of times, if it is not entertaining or meaningful, most viewers start tuning it out. This is our genetic disposition to desensitize. We tend not to watch the ad repeatedly, then suddenly pay attention after a dozen times, and suddenly "get it." The Ipsos ad tracking databases do not support this idea of repetition working well for building ad recall memories or for being effective for motivation and persuasion. Our database of tracked campaigns shows that advertising builds with diminishing returns; each ad exposure has *less* effect.

We can also see the impact of ad repetition (or lack thereof) from users of digital video recorders (DVRs) in the United States. These new DVRs link up with cable TV signals to record hours and hours of TV programming on hard drives. These machines act more like a computer than a typical VHS recorder because the digital signals for TV shows and ads are stored on a computerlike disk drive (not a tape). Users can then easily skip previously recorded programming by a simple push of a button. When we explored the viewing practices of users of these new digital recorders, we learned that a vast majority of consumers skip the TV ads, but they do the skipping more for ads they have already seen and less so for new ads. So when given the choice and the easy technology to skip TV ads, many digital recorder users will still pay attention to the first couple of ad exposures and then work to eliminate the repetition (frequency). Once they get it, they get it. All the more reason for advertisers to make sure the creative is good and not to count on repetition.

## SERVING UP SIMPLE ADVERTISING MEMORY UNITS

Let's revisit those two numbers you were to try remembering a few pages ago. Do you recall them? These are the numbers:

7 0 4 1 7 7 6     6 1 2 1 7

If you do recall them, why? If not, you likely found no relevant meaning or no mnemonic way to recall them. You also likely had no emotional reaction to them; thus, the quality, importance, and meaning of these numbers caused no reason for them to be burned into your long-term memory. In addition, they were not pictorial or in a nice little unit for easy processing by your brain. In a sense, these numbers were presented as a bad advertisement!

But if I gave you these same numbers in a different way, your likelihood of remembering them would increase. The first number is a message for July 4, 1776, Independence Day (in the United States). I put all the numbers together, when this string of several meaningless numbers is just one number (one relatively important and easy to remember date)—month, day, and year:

7   04  1776 = July 4, 1776

The second number is for the word "flag." This is a little more complicated because it is coded by the associated number in the alphabet that spells FLAG (sixth letter, twelfth letter, first letter, and seventh letter). 6  12  1  7 = "Flag"

So now, for Americans in particular, this message (these two series of numbers) has likely become easier to remember, for a few specific reasons:

- You can *picture* the message, with the Stars and Stripes, in your mind.

- This stimulus is relevant to you (if you are American).

- This memory is now represented as one (unified) unit, and not a series of unrelated numbers. The date and flag go together.

- The stimulus is likely to have an emotional set of triggers or associations (childhood memories, fireworks, barbecues, Fourth of July parades, etc.).

I can now imagine that a week from now if you had to recall these numbers, you could do so. It might take you a minute to decode the word flag and arrive at the number 61217, but with this and the Fourth of July date, it would be quite possible for your recall.

As part of my job, I have presented this memory concept in many public speaking events around the world. For each country, I try to use numbers that represent a relevant, important, emotional date for the audience of that country or region. What I find interesting is that even though I did the work myself to find appropriate dates, prepared the presentation, and presented it to a public audience (always a little nervy), I cannot remember the important dates for Mexico, Brazil, Spain, China, Jordan, and so on. I can only say in defense of my poor brain that the chosen dates were not relevant or emotionally charged for me. This matters for memory. Not only is a mnemonic unit filed better in our brains, it also helps the brain if the stimulus is relevant, personally meaningful, and charged with extra senses. As another example of the mechanics of our brain, I can remember the *pictures* I showed as I decoded the numbers into the important dates, and shared a picture of a flag, a key battle, or a conqueror in each of the other countries. I find it totally consistent that the parts I can remember best are the *pictures* and not the dates or numbers. It leverages the pictorial nature of our memory.

## CHAPTER 6 TAKE-AWAY: PUTTING MEMORY TO WORK

The richer and more enhanced the incoming stimulus, the greater the neuronal firing and the better the stimulus will be burned into long-term memory.

- Enriching a brand to appeal to more than just one or two senses will help to create a stronger neuronal burn-in. This enhances the creation of more positive emotional associations for the brand and consideration in the future. Brands that are rich in sensory appeal earn better brand equity.

- Our brain is largely influenced by vision, and we store memories mostly in visual ways. We do not tend to use or see text in our heads. We store memories as units, mnemonics, associations, stories, and metaphors.

- Advertising that leverages a simple storyline, uses mnemonics, or tries to build one thought-unit tends to perform better than ads with multiple cuts in a fragmented video montage.

- Advertising can also work subconsciously, allowing for low attention processing. This is not as strong as advertising that is in the conscious brain and is voluntarily recalled and considered.

- Advertising repetition (frequency of exposure) is a costly way to burn-in a memory. It is likely to be more successful to enrich the advertising with appealing relevant and emotional meaning and only air it for a short while. Soon after, our tendency to desensitize will work to the detriment of the familiar stimulus.

- Presenting a message via visually meaningful mnemonics or icons will leverage how the brain is wired to remember it.

# THE IMPORTANT ROLE OF EMOTIONS

**YOU ARE NOW LIKELY GETTING THE CONCEPT; HUMANS ARE THE PRODUCT** of genetic evolution. We are the way we are for explainable reasons. So why do we have emotions? They must serve a purpose, or they would have evolved away.

## WHAT ARE EMOTIONS?

There are nuances to the definition of an emotion, but they all seem to center on this: an emotion is an experienced mental state as a reaction to something. That is, we have an emotional response to a stimulus. This experienced state is felt to be either positive or negative, and it may cause some physiological changes, such as perspiration, increased heart rates, cold palms, dilated eyes, and flushed cheeks. Emotions can be felt in different levels of intensity as well and can differ in duration.

An emotion or an emotional response does not include attitudes, personal feelings, and personal desires. Just because we can say I feel cold, or

I feel like wearing my new coat to show off, does not mean that these are emotions. Feeling cold is a physical state. Showing off is a desire.

## WHY DO WE HAVE THEM?

The purpose or outcome of an emotional reaction is an inclination to act; whether we do something depends on the nature, intensity, and duration of the emotion, and it depends on how we think about it (our decision-making process). This emotional response and inclination to act (to either take corrective action to get away from danger, or conversely, to seek pleasure) is a survival feature. If we did not develop emotional responses to experience fear and did not have the sense to react to get away from it, our species would likely have died off in the bellies of predators on the plains of Africa, where our ancestors first lived.

In simple terms, we have emotions to allow us to react immediately to danger and also to allow us to consider decisions as being more or less desirable or good. That is, emotions are a part of decision making, and we cannot decide between choices if we did not have emotions associated with each option. How could we decide between choices if we could not judge the choices as good or bad? Thus, rational decision making and irrational emotions are tied together and are not opposites, as once thought. The rational and irrational coexist as two sides of the same coin, not as independent, opposite concepts.

At the most general level, emotions can be classified as either positive or as negative. But we have more words than good and bad to express how we feel—the dictionary has hundreds of useful words for emotions—and we often struggle to perfectly explain how we feel. Many emotions are working subconsciously, and we are not adept at placing a label on them. Although we use our eyes to judge the emotional moods of people around us, research shows that we are not good at recognizing or describing more than about 20 different emotional expressions in other people.

Emotions also work to structure our social interactions. Humans are social beings. We do not operate in isolation from others of our species (like each leopard does); we work in packs or tribes, like other social animals. Admittedly, our cities are big, with many more people than we can interact with and have meaningful emotional connections, but we each form our social circles. We have developed emotional expressions for a reason. We have emotions in order for our socialization to happen. They allow (encourage) us to mate, to keep us together after mating, to help co-raise the offspring, and to reward a healthy lifestyle. Emotions are kind of like the glue of our cohabitation and of our social existence as a species.

We show our emotions both facially and in body language. We have some facial muscles whose only function is to allow us to show facial expressions. These muscles have evolved for the genetic benefit of expressing our feelings to others. Why? By showing our emotions, we are communicating to others. This allows us to get sympathy, to bond over a laugh, to express danger, to assess confusion in others, to avoid threats by detecting anger in others, and so on. In the most basic way, the visual demonstration of our emotions allows us to get along better with fellow humans, and this has been a survival benefit.

## ANIMALS HAVE EMOTIONS, TOO

A summer 2005 issue of *Time* magazine had an interesting article about emotions in animals. Recent studies appear to be supporting the belief that some animals experience states of envy, empathy, and altruism. These beliefs are now becoming mainstream in the world of biology (compared to 50 years ago, when such thinking was rejected). What I find interesting in this work is the reference to the social animals (dogs, dolphins, monkeys, rats) as having the strongest presence of emotions. This is consistent with the evolutionary theory that emotions developed, in part, in correlation with our socialization. That is, we can explain the evolutionary genetic benefit of emotions to facilitate our social cohabitation with others in our species. This relationship between emotions and social skills is not restricted to humans; they help other social animals as well. It is now part of a wider application of the theory of evolution to humans and animals alike.

## THE EMOTIONAL HUMAN

So emotions help us to decide between choices. Every stimulus that enters our brain is tagged with an emotional association, and these entering stimuli and emotional tagging are happening all the time, largely subconsciously, beyond our control. They fill up our brains, and we call on them when we think or act. Our emotions influence our decision making more strongly than our rational thinking between right and wrong and what is rational and smart.

A simple example illustrates the nature of our emotional influences on what could be considered a rational decision-making process. It was February when I was researching the role of emotions and how emotions affected decision making (and motivation). It happened to be the days leading up to Valentine's Day. I think almost every culture celebrates or understands the concept of Valentine's Day. Boys and girls, boyfriends and girlfriends, husbands and wives, and lovers are expected to show their love, usually by buying a card or gift for the person(s) of their love. So off I go to buy something for my wife. But how do I decide what to get?

Naturally, I want the day—and particularly the gift giving—to go well. I want it to be well perceived by my wife, and I want to feel good about all of this for myself, too. I want the gift to be well received so I am thought of (accepted) in a good way. I do not want to blow it such that my wife speaks poorly of me to her friends (and I later hear about it as an object of ridicule at some dinner party). Buying her a power drill for the workshop is out! On the other hand, it would be great if I could excite my wife so much that she tells everyone how wonderful I am: she would like it, and so would I. But I have to consider my male friends, too. If my wife tells all of her friends about the wonderful jewelry I gave her, I might get a few comments from my friends—the husbands—for overdoing it and making them look bad. Husbands do not like being compared to one another by their wives. And of course, jewelry is expensive!

I also hope the Valentine gift meets my wife's expectations. What are these expectations? She doesn't overtly state them, but I can perceive them because I know her. Do I listen or believe her when she says she does not want anything special or expensive? Surely any experienced male knows enough not to believe that.

Because I am a male, I also have certain romantic hopes of my own! So, if I get the right gift, perhaps I can enhance this possibility. Wrong gift, and I might be sleeping with the dog in the doghouse.

But I am also a practical guy. I value efficient, time-saving practices, and I do not like shopping. To buy jewelry downtown requires me to take my car, find parking in an overcrowded city, deal with the uncertainties about how to evaluate jewelry, and so on. These are mostly negative emotional associations for me. On the other hand, I can avoid these problems by walking around the block to the flower store and be back in 15 minutes.

Then, I need to consider if I have bought flowers recently, or for the last several Valentine's Days. I do not want to be too predictable, as if I did not put any thought into the gift. Isn't showing that I made an effort part of the gift? So when was the last time I bought flowers for my wife? Perhaps I should consider something different. But this concerns me, because there is a chance she might not like what I get.

I also consider if I have been good over the past several weeks. Have I been traveling on business, or will I be traveling soon after Valentine's Day? Do I need a gift that will last during my absence while traveling? No—I'll be around, so I can spend quality time with my family. This reduces the need for an exceptionally good gift. Right about now, I am thinking, why do guys stress themselves over such decisions?

Maybe I can buy chocolates. My wife loves chocolates. I've noticed over the past 20 years that she has never shied away from them! I have even learned which ones she likes (dark chocolate with cherry centers). I think a box of chocolates might work this time: flowers are predictable, jewelry has recently been done, and—aren't chocolates an aphrodisiac? Fortunately, there is a good confectionery around the block, and they do a good job of wrapping the box, ribbons and all. Yes, this should work. . . .

Now I need to settle on the size and price. I think my wife is still using the scales and watching her weight since the holiday season. So perhaps a small box—but not too small, that it (me) is perceived as cheap. It must be impressive enough. I am also sensitive to the price in terms of its value. I am blessed with a wife who knows value and avoids overpriced items. So I need to be careful to get good value in my choice. Godiva chocolates are out! But I want to avoid buying a cheap brand because this would reflect poorly on me.

There, I am done. I settle on a midsized box of nice dark chocolate-covered cherries, with pretty ribbons, in a romantic-looking package. I can squeeze this purchase into my lunch break. Perfectly convenient. I make a mental note that next year I might need to buy jewelry, and in the interim, I should keep the flowers flowing . . . not sure this is the best Valentine's gift ever. I am feeling a little stressed, but at least my duty is done and I will not get totally ridiculed. Maybe I should make sure my buddies aren't overdoing it for their wives, so I'm not labeled as the bad husband.

Three weeks later the telephone rings. It is a market research firm calling to conduct a study for Nestlé or Hershey or some other chocolate retailer. "Have I bought a box of chocolates within the past three months?" the interviewer asks. "As a matter of fact, yes," I reply, and I am in the study. The interviewer asks me which brands of chocolates I have bought, and which confectioneries I have visited in the past three months. I tell her brand X. Then she asks, "Why did you buy brand X?" Wow, how do I answer this? Do I tell her about being good recently, about my wife's diet, my friends' wives, my travel schedule, and my hopes of getting lucky—that I bought jewelry for Christmas so I was off the hook for diamonds? No, instead I rationalize. I give a good, safe, helpful answer. I talk about the good characteristics of the chocolates, the dark chocolate-covered cherries, and the nice ribbons on the package.

But my answer is not really correct, is it? It's not wrong, but my rational public answer is quite a small part of the drivers to my purchase. I was largely guided, influenced, and biased by two concepts: emotions and me. What do I get out of this? What do I have to do to get the emotional rewards I want? How did I *feel* about each possible choice I could have made for my wife's Valentine's gift?

In short, this one simple example of buying a gift shows the significant role our feelings and emotions play when deciding what to do. Our emotions directly affect our thinking, our motivations, and our behavior. Many of these feelings are intuitive, personal, and are not to be discussed publicly. These decision criteria are mostly about our expected emotional rewards, not about the features of the box of chocolates. This is what I refer to with the title of this book—Gimme! Our decision-making process, even when buying a gift for someone else, is largely based on our personal and self-centered emotional criteria (what does each possible decision give me?) For advertisers and marketers, we need to recognize the power and nature of emotions and how they affect decision making.

## EMOTIONS AND DECISION MAKING: TWO PEAS IN THE SAME POD

Remember the story of Phineas Cage, the 1850s coal miner with brain damage to his frontal lobe (where emotions are thought to be stored and processed)? This accident did not kill him or reduce his IQ, but due to his reduced ability to deal with emotions, he was less capable of problem solving and making decisions. Why is that?

We have seen that everything that enters our brain transverses the limbic system and is emotionally scored. This emotional association is linked with the stimulus in our memory (perhaps subconsciously). So with each unit of memory we have an emotional feeling to evaluate which we wish to consider. For example, if I consider eating a bowl of strawberry ice cream, the consideration of the pros and cons all have emotional associations or payoffs. The ice cream would be refreshing on this hot day and would make me feel good. On the other hand, I have negative feelings about the ice cream's calories and fat. But I do like strawberries, and I did exercise today. On the other hand, I will be out for a big dinner tonight, so I should hold off. What I am doing as I consider my decision to eat a bowl of ice cream is evaluating all of the emotional associations, rewards, or negative consequences I will experience. Thus, each *rational* decision is bundled with emotional associations and emotional evaluations. These emotional associations are important. If we lacked the emotional elements, we would not be able to make a decision. How could we decide to do something if we could not decide if it will be good or be bad for us? These emotional associations were missing for Phineas Cage, and in turn, he struggled to make good decisions (even though his IQ was unaffected).

In sum, rational decision making is accompanied by emotional evaluations. Sometimes we are more emotional about decision making, and sometimes we are more rational, but nevertheless emotions assist in decision making. Professor Antonio Damasio, in his book *Descartes' Error,* summarizes how emotions cause decision making, and explains that when faced with a decision, we process our decision by asking, "How will I feel as a consequence?" (Descartes had argued that emotions and rational thinking were separate, independent, opposite, and unlinked. That is why Damasio refers to it as "Descartes' error.") Modern learning has taught us that emotions and decision making are tied together. Malcolm Gladwell, in his neat book *Blink,* addresses the concept of that instinctive gut feeling we sometimes have about something. This is the subconscious and emotional aspect of our brain working more quickly to form an opinion than our conscious, thinking brain (as quick as the blink of an eye).

Another example of our emotional subconscious affecting our thinking is the phenomenon of the "bystander problem." This problem illustrates how we react to irrational elements. I first came across this example when taking CPR (cardiopulmonary resuscitation) training 20 years ago. The instructor explained that we would each likely experience someone having a heart attack in our presence at least once in our life. There is an important context (she called it the "innocent bystander" phenomenon) that often happens, which we need to ignore. The innocent bystander phenomenon works this way: the more people witnessing the heart attack, the less likely a person is to help the victim. This is particularly true if we come to a heart attack situation without having been present when it first happened. The explanation behind the innocent bystander phenomenon is one of shared responsibility and thus diminished responsibility for any one person to act. Each bystander starts to mitigate his or her responsibility to act based on the context of others being present. As a group, we reduce or dilute our feeling for a need to be responsible, even if this is not rational and no one is going to the aid of the heart attack victim. If you are the *only* other person present you would act quickly, but not if you are in a larger group. Beware of being an innocent bystander. This is just one example of rational decision making being affected by emotional, irrational feelings.

How many of us immediately evaluate a stranger, or a new person we meet, based on the first two seconds of what we see, hear, and smell? Our senses perceive this person, send a multitude of stimuli to the brain, and we immediately start to emotionally judge whether we like or dislike this person. This is neither right nor wrong. It is natural, instinctive, and how we work. Our emotions and our rational decision making are linked, and they influence each other directly.

I think part of the challenge for each of us is how to recognize where rational thinking stops and starts versus evaluating our emotions and acting on our feelings. Since many emotions reside in our subconscious, we are not great at recognizing them. In addition, when it comes to asking someone why or how he or she made a decision, much of the answer is personal, not likely safe or socially appropriate to share, and perhaps partially subconscious.

A June 2005 article in *Time* magazine caught my attention with respect to our emotional subconscious affecting our behavior. In the Olympic games where players or athletes compete directly against each other (such as boxing), the athletes wearing red are somewhat more victorious than athletes wearing blue. Experts are not sure why this happens, but they believe there are different subconscious associations with red and blue.

Let's review a more pragmatic example about how irrational we can be and how emotions affect our behavior. We conducted a consumer survey and asked people what thoughts, feelings, memories, smells, and so on they associated with McDonald's restaurants. We wanted to explore how much of this was related to the selling messages that come at us from McDonald's advertising. Surprisingly, many people mentioned things that were unrelated to McDonald's actual restaurant, product, or food. Instead, they talked about family members, events, or peripheral elements of McDonald's.

One woman told a story of how the diaper on her young toddler exploded, spilling its contents on the floor of a McDonald's restaurant. She told us she was so embarrassed by this that she refused to go back to that McDonald's. The misadventure of the diaper is not the fault of McDonald's, and yet McDonald's loses out and will not get her future business.

Conversely, an older gentleman told us that it was at a McDonald's restaurant that his son informed him that he, too, had been approved to be a police officer. He thinks positively of McDonald's, with a soft, emotional attachment, always thinking of his son when visiting McDonald's.

So here are two personal stories that have no practical relationship to the rational reasons to choose McDonald's, and yet these associations drive the purchase behavior at this restaurant due to the personal emotions attached to their associations.

It is interesting to note that many consumers talked about the yummy smell of french fries, while others were disgusted by the greasy smell. Others referenced noisy kids' parties or the underpaid staff (often students or immigrants, who are being taken advantage of). Just a small percentage volunteered comments about the Ronald McDonald House. Practically no consumers brought up the rational, functional elements of prices, hours of operation, location, new salads, promotional items, and so on.

So what? We went on in our survey to ask these consumers how they rated their personal associations for McDonald's, and then we reviewed their ratings (favorable versus unfavorable) with their usage and behavioral loyalty with McDonald's. We observed noticeable positive relationship between people's personal associations and their usage of McDonald's.

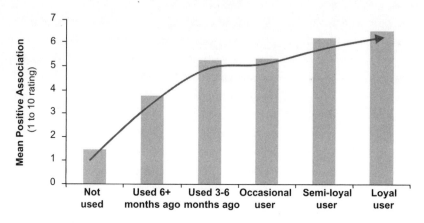

**Fig. 7.1** Rating of Personal Associations for McDonald's X Visits

Consumers who found their personal associations to be positive are more likely to be users of McDonald's. (See Figure 7.1.)

I wonder if McDonald's knows this, and if they take it seriously. Do they know the damage caused by the greasy smell, the movie *Super Size Me,* the belief that their staff are underpaid (and exploited, as one respondent told us), and the omnipresent plastic? These associations are strong and directly affect (override) rational reasons to use McDonald's. Unfortunately, as for the mother with the exploding diaper, some things are beyond McDonald's control. Nevertheless, these personal (not rational) elements drive consumer behavior toward using McDonald's, and this is our key point. Our *personal* associations affect our personal behavior.

## DEATH OF THE ECONOMICALLY RATIONAL HUMAN

Many economists and business thinkers base their models, their explanations, and their predictions on the concept of the economically rational person. That is, people make informed, rational decisions that maximize benefits versus costs. We are supposed to consider the choice of goods or services based on all the costs and efforts we need to follow to acquire them, compared with all the benefits they yield.

As evolutionary biologists, neurologists, and behavioral psychologists learn more about the true nature of humans, we learn that we do not work or think so rationally. We do not find and consider all the facts. We do not like broad choices, so in turn, we tend to consider only a few main criteria. We often make irrational decisions. For example, many of us living in developed nations have tax incentives and investment plans that encourage savings for retirement. These plans are economically advantageous, yet the majority of citizens do not act as economically rational as they should. We do not plan well for the long term. Humans tend to possess better rational cognitive long-term thinking, but in the short term, our thinking tends to degrade toward more emotional, irrational decision making.

Harvard professor David Laibson conducted MRI research with neuroscientists S. M. McClure and J. D. Cohen (of Princeton), and economist George Loewenstein (Carnegie-Mellon University). In their research, they scanned the brain activity of volunteers and found that humans use different parts of the brain for long-term thinking versus short-term thinking (immediate gratification). The short-term or immediate considerations are found more in the limbic system, which is the old brain responsible for more immediate emotional reactions.

Consider a case I heard of a few years ago regarding a movie theater selling two sizes of popcorn: large and small. Approximately 80 percent of the popcorn sales at the theater were for the smaller size, even though the larger size was a better value (in terms of cost per gram). The management of the theater wanted to encourage more sales of the larger size because it made more money in absolute sales. They considered lowering the price of the larger size so as to to improve its value. They also considered increasing the cost of the smaller size to encourage a better value perception of the larger size, but the best outcome was to offer a third size of popcorn even larger than the big size. Even though many customers were not buying the larger of the two original sizes, by offering the third jumbo size, a noteworthy percentage of customers moved to buying what was now the middle size. For some reason, by offering three sizes, customers switched their choice to the middle option. This is not really rational, but it reflects the way humans truly work.

We are also familiar with the pricing of goods and services one cent below the whole dollar—for example, at $5.99 rather than $6.00. More people will buy at $5.99 than one penny could possibly explain. There is something irrational about this one-penny difference.

John Kay, the English economist, discusses the evolutionary nature of mankind and how this explains why economic models fail to apply to communities of people acting in a rational manner. He recognizes that humans

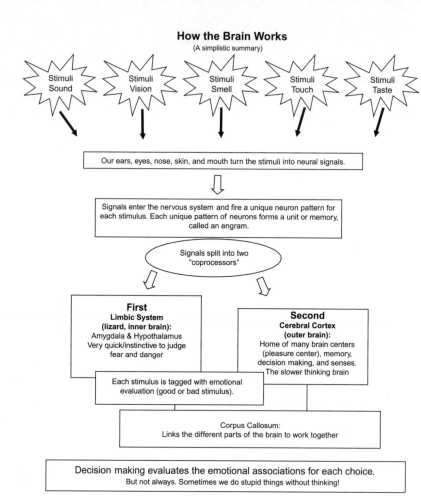

## How the Brain Works
(A simplistic summary)

are social creatures because there are genetically evolutionary benefits in being social. In short, it has helped our species to survive (via shared hunting, shared protection, cooperative raising of offspring, and so on). By being social, we at times have to override our tendencies to be selfish, acting for our own personal benefit over that of the group. By being too selfish, we would likely be kicked out of the social group. Thus we need to be both selfish and social, in a balanced compromise; by being social and cooperative, we will gain. Thus, the purely economically rational person will not always follow the decisions that maximizes his or her own benefits over costs. At times, a person will choose something that is imperfect for him or her because it aids the group, which in turn aids his or her role in the group. This is still explained as being selfish, but the rational economical model is hard to apply in such situations.

Human behavior seems to be better explained through evolutionary biology and behavioral psychology than by the economically rational concept, which is incomplete and too simplistic. For marketers, we need to appreciate the genetic evolutionary basis of the less rational person! To conclude this chapter and to summarize, I plotted a simple summary of how the brain works.

---

## CHAPTER 7 TAKE-AWAY: THE IMPORTANT ROLE OF EMOTIONS

- We have emotions as a consequence of our genetic evolution. They enhance our ability to survive. They allow us to feel fear and to react or retreat. Emotions act as the social glue that allows us to cooperate with others. Emotions equip us with the basic means to make decisions.

- Rational decision making and emotions are linked together and are not opposite ends of a spectrum. They are two sides of the same coin. Every stimulus, event, or experience is judged and tagged with an emotional association. Decision making is about assessing the appeal of these emotional associations.

- Emotional associations do not need to be directly related to the characteristics of the brand or retailer. The associations may be personal—about past experiences, the context of brand use, related to family members, or so on. These personal emotional associations directly affect brand consideration.

- The concept of the economically rational person is dying, because humans do not act so rationally. We need to account for the impacts of emotions and our genetic tendencies when explaining behavior.

---

# CHAPTER 8

# BEYOND EMOTIONS— TO ATTITUDES

WE HAVE SEEN THAT EMOTIONS ARE A NATURAL AND EVOLUTIONARY genetic trait, and we have reviewed how emotions are omnipresent, attached to every little unit of memory. So now we arrive at the point of asking—how does this affect motivations, and what about the cognitive, rational, thinking part of the brain?

Before moving on, let's stop to remind ourselves that the purpose of marketing and advertising is to motivate and to persuade (not just to create emotions). It is important to understand and create emotional associations for brands, but we also need to consider the science of motivation before we can manipulate behavior (sales). There are many studies that show how advertising can influence attitudes, but unless one can activate or trigger the attitudes into action, then the effort is lost. To be clear about this, creating emotional associations is only one part of driving motivation. Advertisers need to think beyond emotional response to get the behavior they want (purchases).

## ATTITUDES AND BELIEFS

Attitudes are a significant motivational factor. If we have a positive attitude toward doing something, we are more likely to do it. Attitudes are defined as the beliefs and feelings toward an event or object. We may have many beliefs relating to any one single object. Earlier I wrote about McDonald's and consumers' associations with them. Many consumers have more than one belief and even have opposing beliefs (some positive, some negative). Some believe the french fries at McDonald's are the best in the world, but they also believe McDonald's exploits student and immigrant labor. Other McDonald's customers dislike the atmosphere of mass production, but they enjoy the idea of the Ronald McDonald House for charitable purposes. That is, for any one element, we likely have many different beliefs and attitudes.

The other component of attitudes is feelings. Not only are our beliefs judged to be favorable or negative for us, we may also have subconscious feelings about the subject. In the McDonald's case discussed earlier, the police officer who learned (while in a McDonald's) of his son also becoming an officer has positive feelings that affect his attitude toward McDonald's. This is not a belief, but a feeling, and this feeling directly biases his attitudes and emotional associations to McDonald's.

So we have attitudes based on beliefs as well as feelings—but what does this matter? The answer is that attitudes, beliefs, and feelings are the decision criteria from which motivation is derived. Marketers need to build and/or support brand attitudes, and if there are many different beliefs or feelings toward the same object, then the proper attitudes need to be heightened.

## DIRECT OR INDIRECT ROUTE TO FORMING ATTITUDES

When it comes to forming attitudes, either we tend to follow a direct route, with considerable engagement of our cognitive thinking, or we tend to follow an indirect, peripheral route. In the direct route, we weigh the pros and cons of the decision. We look at advertising to hear the message and consider it. In a peripheral approach, we form attitudes more by nonmessage cues such as sound bites, public relations, advertising imagery, public opinion, generalizations, the look of things, and so on.

For most purchases we make, as consumers, we tend not to follow the direct route when forming attitudes. Even for high-involvement categories, we still form attitudes based on somewhat peripheral cues. The accumulation of peripheral cues may well be conscious, and they can be quite effective. These cues can also be subconscious. As an example, consider the purchase of a car. As a consumer, we cannot weigh the pros and cons of every car (and genetically, our brains are not conditioned to process so much information). So what do we think about the Kia brand of cars? Personally, I am not so familiar with this brand, but I have some attitudes based on peripheral cues: (1) I know it is not a big mainstream brand, thus, I deduce something based on this fact; (2) I know it is a Korean car company, and this adds a peripheral cue; (3) No one I know drives a Kia car, and this is another bit of information; and (4) I do not recall much advertising for Kia, so I wonder how big and profitable the car company is here in North America. All of these peripheral cues help to form an attitude (fairly or not, rationally or not). Even when directly assessing a car's characteristics, we form irrational opinions based on the sound of the muffler, the sound of the engine, the feel of the car door closing, the new car smell, and so on. Marketing, advertising, and sales all have a role to play in affecting attitudes via peripheral cues, especially when consumers do not often follow direct paths to forming attitudes—especially since humans are emotional, not rational.

## CURRENT ATTITUDES AND FUTURE DECISIONS

Attitudes (and feelings) are built on experiences. They become beliefs over time. As we make decisions and weigh the pros and cons of doing something, we consider our current attitudes, beliefs, and feelings. From this, we imagine our feelings for each possible choice. In a sense, we see in our minds the expected feelings based on experiences and current attitudes. That is, the brain will only lead us to where it can imagine. In completely new, strange, and foreign experiences, we rely on related or similar experiences, beliefs, feelings, and emotions. Even in unfamiliar situations, we try to imagine the pros and cons of each decision. This is why we fear the unknown; in this surrounding, we do not know how to decide or act. This is largely because we can't envision the future.

For advertisers, it is helpful to show consumers a vision for decision. It is often helpful to illustrate or demonstrate the emotional benefits of using the advertised product or service. Consumers see so many commercial impressions a day (some estimate we see over 2,000 commercial or branded impressions a day in North America) that we tend to be lazy in terms of processing them. Thus, it is often helpful to lead the proverbial consumer to the water. We have also learned that creating a favorable attitude is not enough. One must trigger and present the motivation-to-action as clearly and simplistically as possible. These little things can be the all-important tipping point. We will explore this concept of triggering later.

## CHANGING ATTITUDES

The problem with already established attitudes is that they are already burned into one's neurons, and they have emotional attachments or associations. In many cases, they have been present for a long time, and they have been consistently reenforced. Owing to our inclination to be energy efficient, we dislike engaging our lazy brains to constantly rethink things. Thus, changing an established attitude, particularly a negative one, is difficult to accomplish. We are genetically disinclined to change our established attitudes. More fundamentally, our species dislikes change.

In marketing and sales, if one tries to change an attitude or persuade someone, the attitude holder often doubts the intentions of the communicator or questions his or her credibility. Thus, instead of trying to change a stubbornly set attitude, it is often easier for marketers to either (1) alter or leverage other attitudes, or (2) change the importance of the attitude in the holder. That is, if a consumer has a poor attitude toward a brand based on a specific characteristic (for example, the bad aftertaste of a food product) it is likely more fruitful to get the consumer to reduce the importance of this element (reduce the weighting), and to increase the importance of other attributes. For example, for readers who are familiar with Original Listerine mouthwash, and know that it has a strong taste (perhaps terrible!), it is likely better to sell Listerine by creatively packaging the message in a way that says, "We know it tastes bad, but it is this strong sensation that makes Listerine so effective at killing the germs in your mouth." This credibly recognizes a negative attitude toward taste, reduces the importance of taste, and focuses on the importance of killing germs.

Many successful ad campaigns have succeeded by recognizing their brand's shortcomings and admitting or agreeing with the negative attitudes of the consumer. In addition to the Listerine mouthwash discussion, we have seen this same idea work successfully in Canada for Buckley's Mixture cough syrup. Their selling message has been, "It tastes awful, and it works." This works to build greater credibility. It downplays the weight of this attitude (poor taste) and escalates the importance of another attitude (it works). Imagine trying to convince people they are wrong about the bad taste and that it really tastes good. It wouldn't work, because consumers already know about the bad taste.

Another strategy for persuasion in the face of negative attitudes is to add new beliefs. Consumers are less likely to reject or ignore new beliefs that do not challenge existing ones. Beliefs are about attitudes that already exist in the person's mind, so if an original idea is presented, it is unlikely to be met with a preestablished negative judgment. As an example, I read the other day that smoking can lead to impotence in men. Wow—we all know about lung cancer, but impotence is a completely new reason, something I had never considered. It is hard to have a prejudgment about smoking and impotence if this was previously unknown. Only upon hearing this news can someone then try to judge its accuracy and credibility. I can't imagine many men would ignore this fact and then have an attitude that says impotence is fine with me! Thus, offering a new idea is not likely to be met with previously established negative beliefs.

## APPRECIATING CONSUMERS' BELIEFS

Although advertisers do not like to recognize (or promote) the names of their competitors, it is sometimes worthwhile to do so. There appears to be a consensus regarding this, based on many successful examples. If a competitor is obviously superior, much larger, and established, then it is not likely to be so painful to recognize what consumers already know. By doing so, one can match consumers' beliefs, then work to alter the importance of their beliefs. For example, Bayer Aspirin was the first successful, large, mass-distributed pain reliever available to consumers without a prescription. Consumers chose this brand and believed that it helped to reduce pain. Bayer Aspirin became a large, successful brand. Then, along came a new, alternative form of pain reliever—Tylenol. The benefit of Tylenol was that it did not cause upset stomachs or microscopic bleeding in the stomach. Tylenol could recognize Bayer because you couldn't deny or ignore the success of the Bayer brand. The key to Tylenol's success was how it then focused consumer attitudes toward a new belief. Even if most consumers did not experience upset stomach when taking aspirin, it was likely better not to tempt stomach problems and to switch to Tylenol. So, Tylenol went on to great success by telling consumers that the famous Bayer brand might cause microscopic bleeding in your stomach and that Tylenol would not. It was because of Tylenol's great success with this issue of stomach problems that we saw a rash of brands talking about coating their pills and having buffers. Over time, Tylenol was so successful that it dominated and then replaced Bayer Aspirin as the market leader.

When Aleve was introduced, more than two decades later, we saw a similar marketing model as Tylenol. It was easy for Aleve to recognize the popularity of Tylenol, because this wasn't giving Tylenol any benefit it did not already obviously have. So Aleve's ads showed a handful of Tylenol pills and stated that you could either take eight Tylenol per day or take just one dose of Aleve. Again, the advertiser was gaining acceptance, and then working to alter the importance of beliefs to introduce or leverage other beliefs. People, in general, do not like taking medications. Aleve leveraged this attitude in their just-one-dose concept.

Perhaps one of the most famous campaigns to recognize the competitor in its own advertising was Pepsi and its Pepsi Challenge. Coca-Cola was outselling Pepsi by a wide margin (several multiples), and I suppose the folks at Pepsi felt that this was not justified by the taste profiles of the two colas. So along came the Pepsi Challenge. The big idea behind this was that although many people drank Coca-Cola, in a blind taste test many consumers preferred Pepsi. This challenged the whole commercial audience about their beliefs toward Coca-Cola and started consumers thinking of Pepsi in a more favorable manner.

When a brand is strongly outsold by a market leader, it is likely safe to recognize the leader, then work to alter, add, or reweigh the importance of beliefs. What I find interesting is that as brands have named their dominant competitors and then successfully closed the gap on them, they have then stopped directly recognizing the opposition and have adopted an independent, confident leadership tone. Pepsi evolved from the Pepsi taste-test challenge against Coca-Cola into a unique, independent "Taste of a New Generation" campaign. Thus, the concept of recognizing a competitor in an ad campaign, and challenging existing beliefs, is likely best when the sales ratio between the brands is lopsided (and one is only recognizing what the vast majority of the marketplace already knows). Once the gap narrows, when many consumers may no longer hold the ex-leader in such high regard, there should be caution about including the competition in the campaign.

Many successful salespeople say that it is important for a salesperson (and aren't we all trying to sell ideas to others every day) to deal with objections head on. That is, it might be fine to alter the importance (consumers' weighting) of different attributes, but if this task is too difficult, it may be fruitless. For example, if a child does not want to go on a specific ride at the amusement park because he or she feels it is too scary, it's not helpful to ignore it, or tell him or her she is wrong—or to argue "but it is fun," and "everyone else is doing it." This won't reduce the fear. Although this helps a little, it is likely better to recognize the child's fear and deal with it by explaining the safety bars, the padded seats, and how none of the riders are being injured.

Altering or biasing attitudes can also be achieved in subtle and almost indirect subconscious ways. Just small details to context can make a difference in whether attitudes are triggered or recalled. For example, if an upset stomach remedy is perceived as a medicine, and many people do not like taking medication, then perhaps one can alter these brand perceptions. In future advertising, the manufacturer would aim to *not* show the brand in a medicine cabinet or in a bathroom. Instead, it might choose to cast the upset stomach remedy in a beach bag, gym bag, or backpack (things with favorable associations). By altering the context of the brand (away from the bathroom medicine cabinet, toward a more nonmedicinal and fun context), one can alter the beliefs in a subtle emotional way. The intent is to present this brand as a simple, everyday solution that will allow you to get back to normal so you can enjoy your sports, fun, and activities. Any hints of medicine are removed. The packaging should also aim to avoid appearing too medicinal and should have a friendly appearance. These are subtle, peripheral cues, but our senses register them (even if subconsciously), and they can alter our beliefs.

## CHAPTER 8 TAKE-AWAY: BEYOND EMOTIONS—TO ATTITUDES

- To achieve motivation, we need to build on top of emotions. Creating an emotional response to a marketing program is only one (initial) part of driving motivation.

- Beyond emotions, we need to consider the role of attitudes. These are the cumulative set of experiences and beliefs that determine how we feel toward a brand, person, or choice.

- Attitudes toward a brand can be formed from both direct experience and from indirect cues, advertising, sound bites, PR, and so on. Many brands that have not been tried will achieve their brand attitudes through indirect routes (peripheral cues).

- To make a brand decision, we recall our attitudes and beliefs and assess the emotional appeals. We can only assess what we can call up.

- Each choice that we face often has many positive and negative attitudes. It is important for a motivator to emphasize the positive attitudes.

- It is difficult to overcome an established negative attitude. Humans dislike spending the effort needed to change a preset attitude. For advertisers, the need is to alter the weighting put on each attitude and to spin the held attitudes toward the desired motivation or behavior.

# CHAPTER

# 9

# BEYOND ATTITUDES— TO MOTIVATION

**WE HAVE SEEN THAT AN EMOTIONAL REACTION TO A STIMULUS IS A** natural initial response, but our human behavior is more complex, not easily explained by this emotional response. We also hold beliefs and attitudes toward possible choices and toward brands, which build over time and which are due to our experiences. We need to keep exploring to understand how motivation becomes actual behavior. There are still a few more elements before we get to the core concept of "emoti-suasion," and selling to the gimmes.

A common definition of motivation is that it is the driving force (desire) behind the actions we undertake. This is described as an internal state or condition that activates behavior and gives it direction or desire to achieve some goal-oriented behavior. Motivation is based on emotions. More specifically, it is based on emotional rewards or the avoidance of negative emotional experiences. Sometimes we can be forced, manipulated, or coerced into certain behaviors (perhaps even brainwashed), but this type of controlled motivation is not easily achieved and is not readily available as a marketing approach. Instead, a powerful form of motivation is the desire for positive emotional experiences. I think we all appreciate that it is more rewarding and satisfying to do something because we *want to do it* rather than because we *have to do it*. As none of us really has much direct authority or control over others, it is hard to force behavior on others; thus, we need to rely on consumers' own personal desires in order to best motivate them toward a specific behavior.

One of the basics of Psychology 101 is an introduction to Maslow's hierarchy of needs and how this helps explain motivation. This is an important theory about motivation and decision making, but life is more complex than that described by just one simple model relating to needs and satisfying them. Humans also do things based on how they think others will think of them, and we also have our unique personalities, such that two people in a similar situation may act differently.

Let's look at an example to see how these issues work, beyond simple emotions. Imagine walking along a busy sidewalk with some fellow workers during lunch hour, and you see a five dollar bill a few feet away on the street. Your emotional response might be quite favorable. This is better than seeing some sticky chewing gum on the street, or a reminder of someone's dog. This initial feeling is an emotional response. It happens quickly and automatically, and it tends to either be positive or negative—but this emotion is fleeting, as you then start to evaluate what to do (your behavior). Do you stop, disrupt pedestrians, halt your colleagues, and move sideways to pick up the five dollar bill? Your behavior is likely based on how desperate you are for the money and biased by how you perceive your colleagues will think of you for picking it up. If you were with friends and in no rush, you might go for the five dollars, but if you were with business clients, a senior boss, or strangers, you might pass by the money so as to avoid creating an awkward perception of yourself. The decision to act is a cognitive process, beyond the positive initial emotional response to seeing the money. The decision is now based on values and self-perceptions, and different people might react differently due to their personality.

So let's review some of these key concepts of motivation. In a sense, these are the drivers of our behavior: in particular, (1) Maslow's hierarchy of needs, (2) our cognitive styles, and (3) self-perceptions. I think these are all important and help to explain motivation and behavior. *These drivers come into play after our initial emotional response to a stimulus.* Initially, we form an emotional reaction to something—positive or negative—which then works to open up a likely set of behaviors. Then, the specific behavior we follow is biased by our cognitive style (personality), our needs or moods at the time, and self-perceptions. This can be thought of either as a chain reaction or as a multilegged stool, where each leg represents one of these elements, which leads to motivation and behavior.

## MASLOW AND HUMAN NEEDS

Abraham Maslow is best known for his hierarchy of needs. He saw humans as having layers of needs, building upon each other in an ordinal manner. We work our way up a pyramid, building on and passing through each lower stage.

Maslow describes these as needs, and theorizes that we are motivated to seek fulfillment of these needs, in order, from the bottom up. As we satiate these needs they stop being needs. For example, once your thirst is quenched, it stops being a need. Maslow refers to these needs as deficit needs, because they are only motivating needs when they are not filled.

**Self-Actualization**
"to be all that you can be"
e.g., respect, recognition, meaning

**Esteem Needs**
e.g., self-respect, confidence, achievement

**Belonging Needs**
e.g., friends, love (to avoid loneliness)

**Safety Needs**
e.g., a safe protective environment

**Physiological Needs**
e.g., food, water, sleep

As one approaches the top of Maslow's pyramid, our needs become less satiated upon fulfillment, and we may spend a lifetime trying to be the best we can be. Maslow talks about the nature of self-actualization's comprising specific needs. By realizing these characteristics, people can be truly happy. Some of these needs are:

- Truth, honesty, rightness

- Justice, rules, obedience

- To be good, not evil

- Simplicity, to be uncomplicated, effortless

- Humor, playfulness, to be light, alive

- Independence, self-sufficient

- Uniqueness, and to avoid sameness

- Purpose, meaningfulness, and specificity (not by chance, luck, or accident)

Even though this hierarchy of needs is well known, a debate exists as to whether one has to successfully fulfill and pass through each stage to get to the next level. There are examples of people who have only partly met Maslow's definition of esteem but already have interests (and fulfillment) related to self-actualization (the next highest level in Maslow's pyramid). I do not think it is important, for the purpose of this book or for living our lives, to agree or disagree. The purpose of discussing Maslow's work is to understand some of the concepts or ingredients that go into human motivation. The act of pursuing these types of needs helps explain our behavior.

A subset of these higher-level needs is the desire to have *authentic, real* experiences. This idea of authenticity is a common theme in many publications related to behavioral psychology, in marketing books, books about successful brands, and in advertising campaigns (such as Coca-Cola's "The Real Thing"). This came to mind when Andre Agassi was interviewed after a quarterfinal match at the U.S. Open tennis tournament of 2005. A 35-year-old guy, nearing the end of a successful 20-year tennis career, playing his heart out in a grueling five-set match, ending in a tiebreaker in the final set, commented:

> To be honest, with the way a mentality like mine sort of works, this means as much to me as doing it in the finals. This is what it is about. It's about just *authentic* competition, just getting out there and having respect for the other person and letting it fly and letting it be just about the tennis. (*International Herald Tribune,* Sept 9, 2005)

Humans like the real authentic item. This is so important now, with the flood of copycat "me too" brands. There is value and leverage in being the original authentic brand. Many consumers who buy lower-price brands and copycat brands will tell you that they would prefer to buy the real brand if they could afford to. There are marketing opportunities for leveraging the emotional benefits of authenticity.

We also have a desire to *belong.* This is another genetically innate desire. Historically, by belonging to a group, we have enhanced our survival odds. We could work together and benefit from group hunting, from co-raising offspring, by relying on others when ill, and by adding an extra set of eyes to detect danger. Belonging and emotional recognition of one's success also helps us to value life and to keep living. We need to value life in order to get through bad situations. Our social group and feelings of belonging provide some of these emotional gimmes (payoffs). Today, this manifests itself in both formal and informal clubs. As consumers, we can belong with others by sharing common purchases. Perhaps some of the best examples are groups of Harley motorcycle owners, the Porsche Club of America, the fraternity of Apple computer owners, and the feeling of being in a select group with the conspicuous use of an iPod. The desire to belong is an important emotional driver.

We hear from time to time that *necessity* is the mother of invention, but this can't be totally right. It might be true in some circumstances, but I wish I could propose another consideration: "*desire* is the father of invention." Surely, we do not need another type of flavored juice beverage, or another type of breakfast cereal, candy bar, brand of bottled water, pair of shoes, and so on. The constant innovation and introduction of new products is more likely due to *a desire* for a new beverage or candy bar. It is not a *necessity* to have more candy bars or handbags! Desire is a consequence of being human and is what emoti-suasion is all about.

## COGNITIVE STYLE

It is important to recognize that different people process decision making differently. To make a decision, some people rely more on what appear to be emotions, while other people appear to be more rational in their thinking. This is a reflection of their personality. Some people are risk takers, while others prefer safe, sure things. Some people like to stick out as individuals while others tend to be quiet, reserved, and prefer to blend in.

Personality is an important determinant of behavior. An ad that creates an equal level of curiosity in two different people can likely lead to different behaviors from each person, due to his or her personality or disposition. The curiosity created by the ad is the initial emotional response, but the behavior to purchase is a different issue. One consumer may be interested in following up on his or her curiosity, purchasing the product, and experiencing life to its fullest. Another consumer, with equal curiosity, may be reserved, quiet, and risk averse. He or she might first want to ask friends and family if they have tried the new product and may wait until others are all buying it. Thus, with the curious consumer, the desired behavior of buying the brand occurred quickly, while in the latter, risk-averse person there is no sale (different behavior). From the same level of curiosity, we observe two different outcomes based on the personality and cognitive style of the consumers. This example highlights the difference between the role of *personal drivers* and the initial fleeting *emotional response*.

• • •

Instead of describing different types of people, psychologists appear to prefer to describe the different cognitive styles of people. One popular analysis of cognitive styles is the Myers-Briggs Type Indicator (MBTI). This is a set of self-completed evaluations (multiple choice questions about oneself) that are scored so as to define the ways in which we tend to process information and, in turn, how we tend to decide and act. It may be more helpful to evaluate one's cognitive style than to describe one's personality. Our cognitive style may change in different contexts, and we can change or override it. When necessary, we can plan to be more careful rather than emotional or intuitive, but our preferred cognitive style is largely subconscious and is based, in part, on our DNA.

The MBTI self-evaluation test evaluates our cognitive style based on such characteristics as thinking aloud versus keeping one's thinking inside, focusing on details versus preferring to look at the big picture, analyzing facts versus following instinct, and working to conclusive closure versus being an open, flexible, and lateral thinker. Upon answering the many self-assessment questions, the Myers Briggs test describes or classifies one's style of thinking. I have completed the Myers-Briggs self-evaluation as part of a company-wide exercise. We had great fun in an off-site gathering with a Myers-Briggs specialist. We learned about different personalities, through conducting different tasks (such as building a bridge out of Popsicle sticks), and realizing how we each approach decision making in different ways. I believe that one of the great secrets in the world is understanding how others prefer to make their plans and decisions. No one approach is better or worse, and a good team will have a mix, with each style acting as a counterbalance to other styles (to avoid groupthink, all racing off down the wrong decision path, hand in hand). By knowing your style, your spouse's style, and the style of people in your life, you will likely accept them better. You will know how to work or live with them and how to persuade them. Are they a "perceiver" or a "judger"? Are they a "feeler" or a "thinker"? Based on knowing people's cognitive styles, you can adjust how you talk to people and how you offer choices and facts for possible decision making.

In marketing, the selling style needs to match the cognitive style of the target for that context or category. One of the most influential books for me in my early days as an entrepreneur was *The One Minute Salesperson* by Spencer Johnson. To this day, the main message I took from this book was the basic (even obvious) concept of focusing on what the buyer wants to buy and not what I want to sell. In advertising, it is about telling the target what *they* want to hear and not what *you* want to say, and it is about telling them what they want to hear in the approach that best matches their cognitive style.

In advertising and sales, it is important for the communicator to understand the nature of the decision and the nature of the target or persons: is the category largely based on emotional decision making (like beauty products), or based on logical, rational thinking (buying a computer)? Is the target group (or person) largely rational, and does he or she require communication in a more factual way? Or is the target more likely to learn from indirect or peripheral cues (biased by seeing the emotional benefits, with the message delivered in a personal symbolic manner)?

- If a decision is more high involvement and rational, then attack the issues head-on.

- If a decision is more emotional, consider more symbolic and emotional cues.

But always keep in mind that our behavior is based on the pairing of both emotional associations with cognitive thinking. So even for high involvement, rational decision making (e.g., buying a computer or car), there is the real influence of emotions. Consider portable MP3 music players. These can cost several hundred dollars and are easy to describe by various rational features (memory size, battery life, mixing, shuffle functions, and so on), but look at how iPod has dominated this business by selling almost exclusively on imagery and emotions. There are better-equipped MP3 players, yet the emotional appeal of iPods has led to a complete dominance. Every purchase decision, no matter how rationally based it should be, is affected by our emotions. It is genetic, and it matters.

## SELF-PERCEPTION IS A POWERFUL FORCE

The self-perception theory of motivation is based on the concept that we make decisions (partly) based on how we view ourselves and, thus, how we imagine others must be seeing us. "If I do X, or buy brand Y, what will people think of me? My mother, my neighbors, my boss?" For an example of self-perceptions influencing brand choice, consider the beer category. When buying a beer, I have many brand choices. I could choose a brand with a high-quality, artistic image (such as Stella Artois), or I could choose a brand with a harmonistic, male-bonding type image (perhaps a Budweiser), or I could choose an inexpensive price brand. The ultimate choice I make is likely less explained by the product features than by how I think my friends will perceive me. If I am with business colleagues or a client, I might feel Stella Artois is an appropriate choice to be seen ordering, but if it is a weekend barbecue with male friends (for some football and beer), then choosing a Stella Artois would likely draw ridicule. I perceive that my friends will laugh at me and give me a hard time. So instead I choose Budweiser. This is a safe, well-accepted brand. I might only order the lower-priced brands of beer to drink at home, where there is no one around to give me a hard time. I think this simple example illustrates the concept of our actions being driven by self-perceptions and self-centered emotional payoffs (consequences).

This concept of self-perception is a huge driving motivator in what we do in many aspects of life, affecting the clothes we wear, the cars we buy, the brands we are seen with, the friends kids will choose to be seen with, and so many things that are publicly visible. Conversely, I suspect that brands that are *not* seen publicly are not so affected (perhaps self-perceptions are less important for brand choices between cooking oils, baking flour, batteries, underwear, butter, and similar products where the branding is not so obvious to others). For such inconspicuous categories, I propose that personal motivational needs and desires play a greater role.

I have seen consumer research studies for brands of makeup and cosmetics. Once makeup has been applied, the public cannot easily detect which brand the consumer has used. Although the initial decision to wear makeup is likely driven by self-perceptions, the choice *between brands* is likely not. Since the brand of makeup is not obvious to others, the choice of brands for the users is based more on the user's personal feelings, desires, and aspirations. It appears that the emotional drivers associated with makeup have much to do with putting on confidence, individualism, and fun. It appears that looking like a model is not the core emotional benefit. So which brands provide the best feeling of control, confidence, individualism, and fun?

---

## CHAPTER 9 TAKE-AWAY: BEYOND ATTITUDES—TO MOTIVATION

- An emotional response to a stimulus, advertisement, or brand is the initial instinctive reaction, but whether we are motivated to act is often influenced by other elements beyond our emotional response alone:
  —Desires, needs, wants (Maslow's hierarchy of needs)
  —Our cognitive style and personality
  —Self-perceptions and the context: "How will others think of me if I do X?"

- It is more rewarding to do something because we want to rather than because we need to. Motivation is about creating a desire to act on our attitudes. Wanting a brand is a more important driver than needing a brand.

- We have a genetic desire to have authentic, real experiences. We also have a desire to belong. Humans also want personal safety, to experience fun, to have personal success, and so on. These are just some of the many general human desires or needs found in all societies. These can be leveraged as universal motivators. We act to satiate these desires.

- Our unique personality and cognitive style influence our behavior. We have tendencies to be extroverted or introverted, to be analytical or instinctive, and so on. Marketing needs to recognize the nature of its target so as to provide the decision characteristics in the right way.

- Self-perceptions and our relationship in society are key drivers behind our emotions and decision making. The use of many brands will make a social statement about the brand user. In turn, this will drive our motivations to use or not use such brands. This takes the brand beyond its features and characteristics, into the domain of social statements.

# GIMME! GIMME!

**AT THIS POINT, WITH MANY OF THE RAW INGREDIENTS IN MIND (EMOTIONS,** memory, habits, senses, attitudes, beliefs, cognitive styles, moods, and self-perceptions), I hope you are not starting to feel overwhelmed. I became increasingly confused as I first researched motivation. I knew I wanted to understand how emotional response affects motivation, but I had no idea of the complexities involved in getting from the initial emotional response through to truly explaining motivation and behavior. The more I learned, the more I realized that all of these mental elements have one thing in common: our genetic evolution has one primary focal point—our self, our genes.

We are explained by our genes. The core concept of evolution seems to be for genes to reproduce themselves and for the fittest or most superior genes to provide survival advantages over weaker ones. Any genetic benefit that gives an advantage to an organism will aid in the survival of those genes responsible for that specific trait. Thus, genetic evolution, by default, is self-rewarding and selfish. It is about advantages for the genes' future. This is what humans follow in terms of fulfilling needs, desires, and self-perceptions; it's about each of us doing things that we envision being good for ourselves. Survival of the fittest; our value of life is selfish by design, by consequence.

## OUR HEDONISTIC TENDENCIES

*Hedonism.* The word originates from the Greeks, meaning pleasure. A hedonistic person is one who orients his or her life in the pursuit of pleasure. In a manner, our genetic composition means we are all hedonistic, but obviously not in an ostentatious, consumerist manner. In many cultures, hedonism has a negative, self-indulgent, almost immoral connotation, but this is not what I mean by the term. We are not necessarily playboys and immoral in our pursuits, but our genes do lead us to decisions that enhance our survival. Humans everywhere in the world will act to increase pleasure and avoid danger. We do things to increase our safety, to add comfort, to reduce risks, to protect our families, to have fun, to share a laugh, and to make life worth living. This is hedonistic with a small "h." It is our nature of motivation. We do things for our own emotional needs, wants, and desires. Thus, it is logical that if we are genetically wired to be small-h hedonistic, we can appeal to others by satiating their self-centered desires or needs. This is the concept of the gimmes. For marketing, selling, and for influencing others, we are much more effective by recognizing the hedonistic, emotional gimmes in others.

I was on a business trip to Europe that took me out of the home for several days during the annual Canadian spring-cleaning phenomenon. After being shut indoors during our cold, blustery winters, Canadians get this need to do spring cleaning. In a sense, we clean our nest of the clutter that has been building up. This desire happens every year and affects most homeowners. While I was traveling, my wife cleaned the garage, getting rid of unneeded items, reorganizing the rest, and sweeping out the tire dirt. When I returned home, an immaculate garage greeted me. It had obviously been cleaned. I am sure this task was fulfilling for my wife, but it was also useful for me to recognize her efforts and thank her profusely. This further improved her good feelings. Conversely, if I had not appreciated the clean garage, my wife would have been robbed of her chance to get an emotional payoff from me, which would have likely led to disappointment and a cold shoulder. I tell you this to dramatize the concept of satiating my wife's gimmes. As a consequence, I get a warm reception and a big welcome home hug. Now, my wife is not as crass as this, but my stated appreciation gave her an emotional payoff, and in turn, I gained, too. This is emoti-suasion. This is about recognizing, appealing to, and satiating the emotional payoffs for others.

When giving generously to others, even philanthropists are not truly being altruistic; they talk about the good feeling of giving money away. We give our time and our money because we are seen as doing so, we feel connected to society, it gives us a warm fuzzy feeling, we like being thanked by the receiver, there is pressure to participate, we do not like saying no when solicited, and so on. So even when we are being charitable to others, we are doing it for our own emotional gimme. It's about our emotional self, genetically ingrained, through evolution, to lead us through our lives.

The frustration related to these emotional needs, payoffs, and gimmes is that these drivers are largely personal, invisible, secretive, sometimes irrational, sometimes subconscious, and not always thoughtful. The voice in our heads, which talks us into our actions, is self-focused. We are unlikely to discuss what this voice is saying or thinking because our thoughts are often socially inappropriate. We only feel comfortable talking about a few safe, acceptable thoughts. Thus, our emotional drivers are hard to describe, measure, and understand and are rarely shared openly with strangers. Nonetheless, our own conscience, along with our subconscious, our emotions, our habits, our cognitive styles, our personal insecurities, our moods, our self-perceptions, and so on drive us, and the self-rewarding focus of these drivers is the core of what humans are about. This is the focus of emoti-suasion and gimme.

## ASPIRATIONS

Abraham Maslow's work focused mostly on the upper end of his hierarchy of needs. That is, after we satiate our basic needs for food, sleep, and security, we then focus on self-actualization, self-esteem, and personal goals and accomplishments. Much of this is about our striving to be better as individuals, which are our emotional aspirations.

It stands to reason that if we have aspirations, then events, outcomes, and opportunities that allow us to better realize our aspirations must also be of interest to us. That is, aspirations are another form of motivational driver, and brands that fulfill our aspirations should be of greater interest than brands that do not. And if personal aspirations for our own emotional gimme help explain purchase interest for a brand, then we have further evidence that consumers are wired for emoti-suasion. We buy products because we need them (for example, we may need a cure for athlete's foot, a dandruff shampoo, or home insurance), but we also buy brands because we want them (because they help fill our aspirations). Ipsos conducted research to see if aspirations help to explain greater brand motivations or desires and found conclusively that consumers have an interest in brands that meet their aspirations. This will be reviewed in Part 2.

## COMFORT ZONES

Although satiating aspirations may be an effective approach to emoti-suasion, we also found that people express an even stronger desire to stay within their comfort zone. Thus, brands that fit with how people perceive themselves and their world are of greater appeal than brands that are outside of their comfort zone. Naturally, people sometimes reach outside of their comfort zone to aspire to be better or to add novelty to their life, but overall we found that consumers prefer brands within their comfort zone; the closer a brand matches how consumers perceive themselves, the greater the purchase interest. People buy brands for their self-perceptions and emotional payoffs much more than by assessing the product's characteristics, package size, and price.

One specific implication of comfort zones is that brands can be sold based on their values rather than just their product or service features and functional benefits. Many successful brands have evolved from an initial definition of their brands based on a tangible product or service feature toward a brand definition based on values. Nike, for example, is a brand that is now better defined by a value ("Just do it") than a tangible feature in its sporting goods line. Not only do values appeal to humans, but also these intangibles are harder for price brands and generic products to copy.

## INCENTIVES

Many corporations offer publicized employee bonus programs to encourage and reward the desired behavior of employees. These are visible, obvious, and well-described incentives that employees can focus their behavior on to achieve, often with monetary payoffs. We also have frequent flyer loyalty programs, retail loyalty programs, and many brand promotions that encourage repeat or multiple package purchases. We also have many personal, less obvious incentives: namely, emotional payoff incentives: "If I do X, I hope to get a payoff of Y." If a child cleans his room, he hopes to get his mother's approval; if a young man is successful in his career, he hopes to earn his father's respect as an equal.

Steven Levitt talks about this in his book *Freakonomics*. Levitt is a trained economist, but much of his research has been applied to answering uncommon questions. He, along with Stephen Dubner, write about some of the observed behaviors of Sumo wrestlers, drug dealers, schoolteachers, and television game show players, among other somewhat offbeat groups. Levitt shows how people's behaviors are often explained by finding the core personal incentive. There are many interesting studies in *Freakonomics* that support the motivational concept of our personal gimmes.

One group Levitt researched is real estate agents. He presents powerful insights into how the real estate agent selling your house is often not incentivized to truly maximize the selling price for you—real estate agents' behavior follows the personal incentives that best reward them. The commission a real estate agent earns for selling a home is weighed against his or her cost of advertising the home and showing it, as well as the additional demands of waiting for a possibly better offer to arrive. Is it really worth it for the agent to get an extra $10,000 for your house if they only net about $150 more in commission for doing so? Your agent likely doesn't think so! But when it comes to a real estate agent selling their own house, when they get both the $150 commission and the extra $10,000 to the selling price for their house, they are more likely to wait for a better offer.

We should also recognize that some of these perceived incentives are hidden, unclear, and may be perceived as irrational by others. In the fall of 2005, several different state lotteries' jackpots escalated dramatically. The jackpot for such a lottery, often called "Powerball," carries over to the next draw if there is no winner. In turn, as more tickets are purchased, the jackpot increases, with a few jackpots exceeding $250 million. The chance of any ticket winning a Powerball is about one in 146 million, and the odds don't change with each drawing, but when the jackpot gets to such huge levels, consumers line up for hours outside corner stores that sell lottery tickets. They don't line up when the jackpot is $50 million, as if winning $50 million wouldn't improve their life. It doesn't seem rational. As has been said by many psychologists, we act on emotions and then rationalize with cognition.

To summarize, we all have our incentives, and they are often emotional, personal, subconscious, self-rewarding, and not fully explainable. They are powerful, and they are focused on the self, not on the company incentive program, not on the lottery, and not on the functional characteristics of a product or service. Advertisers need to sell the specific emotional gimmes that consumers seek rather than focusing on product features, service characteristics, and other external, impersonal elements that lack emoti-suasion. Advertisers can reference the physical features of the brand as support or license to believe, but the features themselves are not what drives motivation or behavior. Many marketers appreciate the need to be consumer-centric, but many marketing programs are still brand focused, such as with the current trend in holistic brand communication planning, which still refers to how the many different touchpoints contribute to the brand rather than to emoti-suasion. The question we are always asking ourselves is, "What does this brand or choice give me?" Marketers and all people wishing to motivate others need to help consumers answer this question.

## CHAPTER 10 TAKE-AWAY: GIMME! GIMME!

- We are explained by our genetic traits. Genetic evolution, by its nature, is self-rewarding. In turn, it stands to reason that humans are genetically designed to be selfish.

- We do things for our own emotional needs, wants, and desires. Thus, it is logical to appeal to others by aiming to satisfy their self-centered emotional desires. This is the concept of emoti-suasion. Marketing efforts that address emotional gimmes will be well regarded.

- Humans have aspirations (to be better, more outgoing, and so on), and these can be strong drivers behind our motivations and behaviors.

- We also have our comfort zone and, as much as we aspire to be better, we do not drift too far out of it very often. People buy brands that fit with their own values and personality; thus, brands can be sold based on values rather than product or service features.

- Incentives are all around us, including tangible loyalty reward programs and intangible emotional incentives (like earning approval from others). These incentives may be hidden, quite personal, and even subconscious; nonetheless, our behavior is often influenced by them. Brands can help to satiate emotional incentives.

# CHAPTER 11

# EMOTI-SUASION

**MOTIVATION APPEARS TO RESEMBLE A MULTILEGGED STOOL, NOT A SINGLE** chain of brain activity, but rather a combination of various brain processes. It involves different parts of the brain, it combines emotions and senses with cognitive thinking, and it is largely biased by our genetic composition, which influences how and why we do what we do.

What does this mean today, for consumerism and marketing? When deciding about brand purchases, we assess all of the mental and emotional benefits for ourselves. We consider what the brand represents, what it promises, plus the associations we have—then we decide if we want the emotional payoffs the brand offers. If a brand has weak emotional associations or payoffs, it is unlikely to be so well considered.

On the other hand, we have already discussed how having the right brand associations and attitudes may not be enough. In order for motivation to be influenced by brand associations, consumers need to activate and call up these associations at the right time, envisioning the outcome and payoffs of choosing the brand. The mind will only lead the body to where it can see. We have two important concepts to cover to finally activate motivation and behavior: expectancy theory and triggering. Both are influential and are highly affected by marketing programs.

## EXPECTANCY THEORY

Expectancy theory (from Victor Vroom) is the concept that decision making is based on what we *envision* as the payoffs of each possible choice. That is, for each possible decision, we have an expectation of the pros and cons, which we then consciously and subconsciously evaluate in order to make a decision. Thus, it stands to reason that our decision-making process is only based on what we can see or expect. If we have forgotten related facts, or fail to call up the right associations, then these missing pieces may have only a minor subconscious influence or none at all. It is important for any person trying to motivate another that the target has the motivator's positive visions and biases in mind. The motivator must work to activate the preferred attitudes and to help the target see the positive emotional payoffs of the desired behavior, as sports coaches do for elite athletes. Similarly, this is what advertisers can do for consumers. Step one is getting the brand associations into the consumer, but of equal importance is activating these associations for the brand at the right time.

Our expectations are often what lead to our being happy or disappointed. Smart market researchers have learned that when asking people about their satisfaction related to a product or service, such as a hotel stay, they also have to ask about expectations. As consumers, when deciding whether to stay at a four-star hotel or a two-star hotel, we evaluate factors such as the price versus the expected service of the hotel. We expect more from a four-star hotel than we do of a lesser two-star hotel. If we select the four-star hotel, we may be disappointed (and even angry) if it does not deliver to our expectations. The four-star hotel may still deliver better service than the two-star hotel (the room may be bigger, with a nicer television, and be quieter), but we could still be less satisfied with our stay at the four-star hotel because we expected more than it delivered. Since our expectations of the two-star hotel are lower, we could be easily satisfied with a much lower level of service.

Consumers often have two different types of expectations: we have an expectation about what is likely to happen, and we also have an expectation about what should happen. For example, I might expect to wait 20 minutes if I go to buy stamps at the post office, but I feel I have a right to expect just a 5-minute wait as the maximum anyone should experience. That is, five minutes is a reasonable expectation.

This concept of expectancy is not likely new for readers, but what strikes me as insightful is the heart of this: the selfish, self-centered human. We evaluate things in life at a core personal level, against our own expectations. Do we really have the right to be upset with a stay at a four-star hotel? Surely, in absolute terms, these hotels offer some of the best or highest qualities. Nonetheless, the level of disappointment and the number of complaints is just as high for four-star hotels as for one-star hotels, where perhaps there are real material concerns! Aren't Mercedes-Benz owners just as dissatisfied as owners of Kias? J. D. Powers and Associates, a U.S.-based research firm with expertise evaluating cars among owners, appears to recognize mid-price and low-price cars for driver satisfaction as much or more than for higher-end cars. In a July 2003 press release from J. D. Power & Associates, Toyota was ranked the highest for customer satisfaction in Germany, ahead of BMW, Mercedes, and Audi.

In my previously described case of buying a Valentine's Day gift, I considered several sets of available attitudes: (1) diamonds are beautiful and wonderfully romantic; (2) diamonds are really expensive; (3) I am suspicious of the diamond retail business; (4) chocolates are fun and romantic; (5) I hate trying to find a parking spot downtown during the day; (6) I like flowers in my house; (7) going out for dinner is easy to arrange; and so on. As I think about what to buy for Valentine's Day, I consider all of these attitudes and associations. A marketer would want to be sure that I had their brand in mind and a preferential vision of their emotional payoffs (whether for jewelry, flowers, chocolates, or a restaurant). Customers must envision the emotional payoff of using the brand in order to be motivated. If we fail to call up the brand associations at the right time, then they will fail to be considered. Thus, in order to drive behavior, marketing has two key roles: getting the right brand associations into consumers and *activating the right associations at the right time.*

Sometimes we do things based just on emotions and attitudinal evaluation without cognition. We sometimes forget to think. We act on instinct, or we act too quickly, based on our subconscious emotions, beliefs, values, and attitudes. Expectancy theory is not just based on rational cognitive thinking; our emotions, our subconscious, and our genetic evolutionary traits come into play as well.

Let's also recognize that many advertised products and services are familiar to consumers. Many mature brands have existed for 20 plus years, and consumers already have established attitudes and associations toward these brands. The challenge is no longer to build attitudes and beliefs about the brand. Instead, the future success of advertising for such brands will be based on triggering (retrieving, activating) the established attitudes into action.

## TRIGGERING

Much advertising around the world fails to recognize the importance of triggering. We have seen that having the appropriate consumer attitudes is not enough. In addition to building desired attitudes in consumers, we need to trigger these attitudes to influence motivation more strongly. We need to activate people enough so that they call up and strongly consider our desired attitudes.

In North America, there is a popular brand of cereal named Kellogg's Raisin Bran. Practically every cereal eater knows the brand's advertising campaign: "Two scoops of raisins in Kellogg's Raisin Bran." It's been a consistent advertising positioning for more than 20 years. We understand this. But what this campaign fails to do is trigger this raisin benefit at relevant times (when it matters), with an emphasis on positive beliefs and emotional rewards. What are the emotional benefits of lots of raisins in my bran flakes cereal? When should I be thinking about these attitudinal or emotional payoffs? The ad campaign needs to evolve into emoti-suasion, with triggers.

A great example of a successful campaign that used triggering well is Miller beer's "It's Miller Time." Most North American adults over 35 years of age know the slogan and its implications. To this day, despite the end of the campaign years ago, people understand "It's Miller Time." Miller's campaign leveraged the concept that after a hard day's work, it was time to relax and enjoy a beer. It is an emotional transition from work to relaxation, a beer category consumption time, and Miller took ownership of it. The Miller brand is triggered in our minds by relating itself to this happy hour. The

Miller campaign beautifully captures this in an easy-to-remember slogan that activates positive feelings of quitting work, triggers the beer consumption period, and ties in the brand name, all in one easy-to-remember memory unit. "Miller Time" is a great example of triggering the attitudes and the brand at the relevant time association.

In the early days of the market research company that my business partner and I owned, we conducted consumer research for the Canadian government. Specifically, we worked with the health department on anti-smoking and responsible drinking advertising. For both initiatives, the challenge was not really to create the desired attitudes in people. Smoking is unhealthy and drinking and driving is dangerous. We all know this, believe it, and feel badly about it, but people continue to smoke and people continue to drink before driving. This is a prime example of the difference between having the right appropriate attitude and being able to activate or trigger the attitudes for the desired behavior. Persuasion is about both creating the attitude and triggering these attitudes at the relevant time; it is about triggering the right attitude, because we often have several beliefs (likes and dislikes) associated with each stimulus. For example, a smoker has both negative associations and positive associations related to smoking. It is important to trigger the right relevant attitudes and increase the weight of these in the person's decision-making process at the point when the person is considering his or her next cigarette.

Sometimes the trigger can be subtle. Malcolm Gladwell, in his book *The Tipping Point,* describes a study by psychologist Howard Levanthal with students at Yale University. Levanthal wanted to assess how to persuade students to get a tetanus shot. In particular, Levanthal wanted to study the effects of "high fear" versus "low fear" messages. He divided students into two groups and gave each group a different booklet. One booklet used dramatic language, pictures, and high fear content to persuade students to be inoculated against tetanus (free at the campus health center). The second booklet also encouraged inoculation, but was toned down. This booklet was just as informative, but lacked the provocative pictures and high fear. Predictably, the group of students getting the high-fear booklet was more convinced of the dangers of tetanus and was more likely to say they were going to get a tetanus shot. Despite the stronger attitudes and persuasion from this one group, one month later just 3 percent of the students had gone to the health center for their shot. It was the same level for both the high-fear and low-fear groups. Thus, the emotional response and motivation was higher in the high fear group, but the behavior (getting inoculated) was no different between the two groups. This is the difference between establishing the desired emotional and attitudinal reactions versus motivation and behavior.

Intrigued by this outcome, Levanthal went on to repeat the same experiment, but made one small change to the booklet, he included a campus map with the health center indicated and the hours the tetanus shots were available. This extra element increased the inoculation rate to 28 percent from the high-fear and low-fear groups equally. As university seniors, most participants in the study already likely knew where the health center was. The difference of adding the map and the health center's hours was an extra trigger beyond the attitudes. The differences between the high-fear group and the low-fear group were negligible. The observed behavior of being inoculated was about the same between the two groups, and much higher than in the first study (without the map and without the hours of the health center).

This example illustrates the difference between attitudes and actual desired behavior. Although one group was initially more motivated than the other, there was no difference in behavior. In order to get the desired behavior in marketing or advertising (namely, sales), marketers must further understand and leverage more about what makes humans do things.

## THE MOODY TARGET

Targeting is a core concept in marketing. Understanding the nature of the target helps to develop the selling message. Consumers are moody creatures, though. Our emotional needs, desires, and energies change from day to day; thus the nature of customer targets is changing daily. Here today, gone tomorrow, and back again next week. We can see this by the brands consumers use. In many categories, consumers are rarely loyal to one and only one brand. Often we buy different brands over the course of the year, due to our changing emotional needs—one situation might be satiated by drinking Stella Artois, while the next day the need calls for a more harmonised, masculine beer like Budweiser. Often consumers' patterns of brand choice do not group common brands, but include different brand profiles.

That is, if a beer drinker is going to consume several different beer brands, the set of brands is not likely identical in imagery, emotional associations, and gimme payoffs. Instead, we often find sets of different brands consumed for different emotional purposes or needs.

Perhaps a helpful way to think of these emotional drivers is as buckets of water, one bucket per emotional driver. We each have many different emotional buckets, at different sizes, with different levels of water in each. As we live life, each event adds water or uses up water in our emotional buckets. For example, if I was to take a vacation with a friend, doing uniquely adventurous, fun activities (scuba diving, sailing, wind-surfing, and so on) then I would likely be adding water to a couple of my emotional need buckets, namely my pleasurable feeling bucket and my fun and excitement bucket, while also using up water from the safety and avoiding risk bucket and the family harmony bucket. Then, after a week of vacation, I return home. If I was to be called by a friend to go to a pub for beer and watch a football game, I might be motivated to say no because I have recently run down my family harmony bucket. I would likely wish to stay home and spend time with my wife and children to add to my harmony bucket. In turn, I start to run down my fun/adventure/excitement bucket (which I just overfilled while on vacation the previous week). Everything we do is adding or deleting units of satiation against our personal needs or desires.

We each have different levels of equilibrium for our buckets of desires. We are motivated to achieve equilibrium in our own buckets for whatever size buckets we have and whatever water level we desire. As a bucket gets out of balance, we get motivated to restore the balance. We respond better to events that satiate that emotional need. The more the bucket gets out of equilibrium, the more likely we are to want to rebalance it.

We are often described by the nature of our buckets. If a person has a big bucket for fun and excitement and is constantly working to add water to this bucket, we might describe this person as a party animal or adventurer. A curious thing, and perhaps even a complicating factor for marketers and sales people, is that party animals do not consistently look for fun and excitement. Sometimes these party animals do reserved, quiet events. Conversely, sometimes reserved, harmonious people do adventurous outgoing things. This reflects their moods and their efforts to satiate different emotional desires as they ebb and flow. This makes marketing complex, because how do you target and sell to constantly evolving, moody consumers?

In our ad-testing R&D, we discovered that many ads that were scored or evaluated by consumers as being of one mood or style were not always of interest to people of that style. For example, an ad that was adventurous and gave greater perceptions of adventure was not always persuasive to those who described themselves as being adventurous or aspired to be more adventurous. The problem is that moods change and we respond differently toward brands, differently toward people, and differently toward events, based on our emotional needs.

The implication is that marketers should not aim to sell to a certain target or worry about the mood of the consumer. Instead, it is about the brand and building associations *on to the brand*. Consumers change moods daily, but brands endure throughout. If consumers had a clear understanding of the emotional associations for each beer brand, then, when in a given mood, they know which brand will satiate their emotional desire. For example, if Stella Artois beer has associations of prestige and being pleasurable, and Budweiser has associations of harmony or fitting in with the guys or traditional values, then depending on one's mood, the same one beer drinker can choose Stella Artois when they want to treat themselves, or they can pick Bud when they want to fit in. And if they wanted an escapism and adventure, they might select a Corona or other beer from some exotic vacation destination.

Audi and Volkswagen have a business alliance of sorts. They work together, but they also have different brand imagery. I find it interesting how similar the Audi A8 model is to the VW Phaeton model. Both cars have powerful eight-cylinder engines, similar appearance, nicely decorated interiors, and price tags of about $67,000 to $69,000 U.S. So why do Audi and Volkswagen have two similar products with different brand names? Perhaps to allow the buyer to experience different emotional payoffs. Or, in the eyes of the consumer who has decided to buy this class of car, they can then choose between the emotional associations of being seen in an Audi or being seen in a VW. Reserved or image-conscious people who wish to avoid attention might wish to select the VW Phaeton versus the Audi. Those who want the feeling of safety and success might wish to select the Audi. The choice between brands has little to do with the rational cognitively tangible characteristics of these two cars. It is about self-perceptions, emoti-suasion, and the emotional gimmes.

This brings up a debate about segmenting people by emotional profiles. I am in favor of segmenting consumers into ideal targets who are more likely to be open to and persuaded by an advertiser's selling message, but marketers should not think of them as unique, separate groups. First, there is no real cost-effective method for mass marketing to just one unique target at a time, and, more important, it is often too limiting to the marketer to focus on many small segments with individual messages. Instead, I think marketers are better served by appealing to emotional needs in all of us, rather than trying to appeal to the dominant emotional needs of a subsegment. For example, Volvo has been working to create a safety image for their brand. I doubt that Volvo is interested in only targeting the group of people who are interested in safety. This is too restrictive. Instead, Volvo is appealing to the need for safety in everyone. We all have this emotional need, just at varying levels. A good marketing effort might even sell to someone with just average interest in safety, as long as other elements of Volvo are satiating other emotional needs as well (for example, executive image or good environmental practices). Even if a particular consumer is not interested in Volvo or safety, it serves Volvo well to have consumers know this, because word-of-mouth between friends and family is a strong influencer on brand choice.

So let's recap. Attitudes need to be built in peoples' minds with positive (desirable) emotions. To motivate behavior, marketers need to trigger and affect how these attitudes are called up. The successful marketer needs to do the following:

1. Create the appropriate attitudes and emotional associations *for the brand*.

2. Support or alter the weighting toward the desired associations (among the many pros and cons).

3. Build the relevant *triggers* to call up and activate these emotional associations at the right time.

This brings me to a revised (simple) summary of how to explain motivation and behavior.

# MODEL FOR MOTIVATION

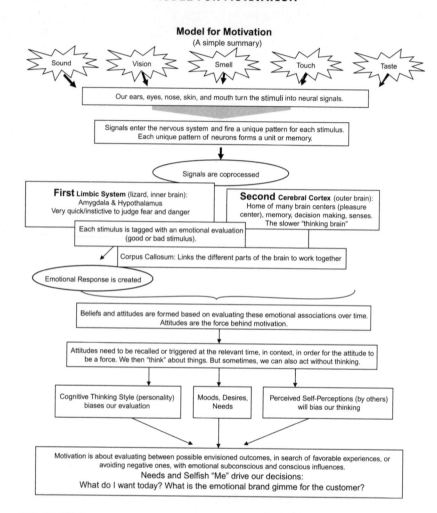

**Model for Motivation**
(A simple summary)

Sound | Vision | Smell | Touch | Taste

Our ears, eyes, nose, skin, and mouth turn the stimuli into neural signals.

Signals enter the nervous system and fire a unique pattern for each stimulus. Each unique pattern of neurons forms a unit or memory.

Signals are coprocessed

**First** Limbic System (lizard, inner brain): Amygdala & Hypothalamus Very quick/instictive to judge fear and danger

**Second** Cerebral Cortex (outer brain): Home of many brain centers (pleasure center), memory, decision making, senses. The slower "thinking brain"

Each stimulus is tagged with an emotional evaluation (good or bad stimulus).

Corpus Callosum: Links the different parts of the brain to work together

Emotional Response is created

Beliefs and attitudes are formed based on evaluating these emotional associations over time. Attitudes are the force behind motivation.

Attitudes need to be recalled or triggered at the relevant time, in context, in order for the attitude to be a force. We then "think" about things. But sometimes, we can also act without thinking.

Cognitive Thinking Style (personality) biases our evaluation

Moods, Desires, Needs

Perceived Self-Perceptions (by others) will bias our thinking

Motivation is about evaluating between possible envisioned outcomes, in search of favorable experiences, or avoiding negative ones, with emotional subconscious and conscious influences. Needs and Selfish "Me" drive our decisions: What do I want today? What is the emotional brand gimme for the customer?

## CHAPTER 11 TAKE-AWAY: EMOTI-SUASION

- In order for motivation to be influenced by brand associations, consumers need to activate and call up these associations at the right time. Consumers must be able to envision the outcome and payoffs of choosing the brand. The mind will only lead the body to where it can see.

- Marketers must work to activate the preferred attitudes and to help the consumer see the positive emotional payoffs of the desired behavior.

- Expectations are what support our decision making. Expectations also determine our satisfaction (or not) with the decision. Did the decision live up to the expectations?

- Many brands, products, or services are familiar to consumers. Consumers already have established many brand attitudes and associations in their heads. So, going forward, the success of advertising for such established brands relies *on triggering their established attitudes* into action.

- Humans are moody creatures. Our emotional needs, desires, and energies change from day to day. Thus, the nature of the customer target is changing daily.

- In turn, marketers should not focus on the target specifically, but instead should be building the emotional associations and values *for the brand*. It is the brand that is purchased to satiate the emotional gimmes of a consumer who is in a particular mood at the time.

PART 2

# LESSONS LEARNED AND FOLLOWING OUR GENETIC WIRING

# CHAPTER

# LEARNING FROM IPSOS CONSUMER RESEARCH

**AT IPSOS, THE CORE OF OUR PHILOSOPHY ON EFFECTIVE ADVERTISING** focuses on the capability of advertising to break through with correct brand attribution and then to persuade, or motivate, or support brand equity, or all three. The role of advertising is neither to merely entertain nor to communicate: the ad must do something for the brand. Our clients hire us to help achieve effective advertising that drives brand sales and brand equity. Entertainment and messaging are just contributing elements.

Advertising best practices follow the evolutionary characteristics of mankind. By studying the Ipsos research data, we find ample proof. In addition to its aesthetic value, there is a real, true science to advertising. Understanding the human sciences helps us to be better motivators and advertisers.

I believe you will find convincing proof in the following pages that advertising and brand management follow the traits of human evolution. Part 2 discusses the nature of advertising and brand management as a business and shares the best practices as gleaned from Ipsos data. From thousands of ad pretests, in-market ad trackers, and brand equity assessments, we extracted these facts to help advertisers skew their odds of advertising success.

I do not intend to take you through the gory details of all the research itself other than the minimum amount necessary to understand the learning. I think you will find that our learning will help increase your appreciation of the best practices of advertising.

- What do emotions contribute to motivation?

- How do personal associations influence motivation?

- How do personal needs, desires, and wants affect motivation?

- How do our brand senses contribute to brand desire?

- How does advertising work?

## ADVERTISING IS A BUSINESS

*Half the money I spend on advertising is wasted; the trouble is,*
*I don't know which half.*

—JOHN WANAMAKER, department store retailer (1922)

Mr. Wanamaker's legendary statement is likely as true today as it was when he said it a hundred years ago—but it doesn't have to be the case. Today, we know much more about how advertising works. There is ample proof that advertising motivates and drives greater sales. Still, less than half of the ad campaigns in Ipsos' database achieve their goals.

For an industry that is supposed to lead and cause change, the ad industry has not evolved since Mr. Wanamaker's time. Despite the knowledge gained over the past 75 years, many advertising practices are money wasters—but this should and can change if we make the effort to learn the lessons in front of us. As Santayana said, those who cannot remember the past are condemned to repeat it. In addition, we have a new understanding about how the brain works, about our genetic evolution and about motivation. Combining old knowledge with new understanding is what will lead to more effective marketing and motivation.

In discussing advertising management, we need to recognize that this is a business—a serious business, with over $350 billion U.S. dollars spent globally on advertising. Manufacturers and service providers are not advertising just for the art of it: it is both an expense and an investment in the future, and it should be critically perceived as such. In order to manage this business of motivation, we need to measure it, as it's difficult to manage something you don't measure and understand. So we need to make concerted efforts to reduce the risk of failure, even if some feel this turns the art of advertising into more of a science. It's too costly to fail, and it's too risky to rely on the judgment of a few experts, who may be wrong.

The rest of this book is dedicated to some of the lessons we have observed from our databases at Ipsos. By virtue of a specialization in advertising research over the past 30 years, Ipsos ASI ("The Advertising Research Company") has accumulated unprecedented databases of tested ads, tracked in-market ad campaigns, and assessed brands' equity. The key to these databases is our practice of following a common philosophy for each study we conduct for advertisers and ad agencies. In turn, we can align the thousands of studies to detect patterns of how effective advertising works and why poor advertising fails.

To be clear, these learned lessons are not one person's theories. These are factual, observed patterns of humans at work; real, undeniable facts about the science of advertising. By following these understandings, advertisers are likely to reduce the risk of failure in their marketing efforts. Obviously, there are exceptions and examples of an ad or an advertising campaign that rebuts each lesson learned, but when it comes to risk management, it is prudent not to bet on the exceptions.

## MANAGING THE ODDS

Our leading advertising pretests (Next*TV and Next*Idea) are accurate about what will actually happen in-market about 80 percent of the time. For marketing dollar risk management, this means we have a 20 percent chance of killing a good idea (which might have gone on-air and done a good sales job) versus an 80 percent chance of preventing a bad ad from being used. The cost of killing a good idea means the ad agency has to find another one. For this, I truly apologize. But the four-in-five odds of preventing a bad ad from being used can save considerable amounts of money— millions!

Creativity is king. It is critical to have good, strong, advertising creative to maximize the use of media dollars: airing weak or just average creative is a poor investment. To encourage creative excellence, an advertiser needs to set up an appropriate ad pretesting system and allow time for the process to succeed. Too often, we observe that time runs out for the ad agency to develop great ads. As the deadline approaches for when the ads need to be sent to the media companies, we see companies compromise the quality of produced creative. Perhaps this is one of the biggest challenges in the advertising world. To increase the odds, ad agencies should be asked for five good ideas. Then these ad concepts should be pretested with consumers, since it is their judgment that matters, not that of a few marketing executives. Marketing experts are poor judges of good advertisements (as evidenced by much in-market failure). We can increase the odds of finding a great ad idea if we develop more than just one best recommendation from the ad agency. This is risk management, with an effort to improve the odds. The payoff is immense.

Part of managing the odds also starts at the beginning, with an appreciation about how humans tick, how good advertising works, and how to avoid pitfalls. The majority of Part 2 deals with sharing some of the lessons learned to help skew the advertiser's odds toward success.

## BRANDING MATTERS

Economic evaluations of corporations show the difference between the value of the company's market capitalization and the value of the company's factories and assets. For example, in 2005, the value of all of Coca-Cola's stocks was about $100 billion (U.S.), but its book value was only $16 billion. This difference reflects, among other things, the economic value of the *brand* named Coca-Cola. If this company made generic or private-label beverages, it would unlikely have the same stock value. This is the power of the brand. This power comes from the desire of consumers to want to choose Coca-Cola over other brand choices, even at a higher price than others. It is this brand power that allows Coca-Cola to earn consumer loyalty, charge a premium price, and earn greater ongoing profitability. Procter & Gamble is perhaps one of the best-managed and most successful manufacturers of branded, fast-moving consumer goods. In 2005, P&G had a similar book value to Coca-Cola at $16 billion, but it had an even higher market capitalization level at $142 billion. This reflects their very strong brands.

To the consumer, this economic value and financial goodwill on the balance sheet of Coca-Cola or P&G means little. What is the benefit to the consumer? The answer is that branding reduces one's risk when choosing a product. By identifying and selecting a familiar brand, we avoid the risk of disappointment; the right decision can lead to many positive emotional payoffs for the consumer. As we have seen, brand choice and the emotional payoff is at the core of personal motivation. So how does the brand manager create and drive this set of consumer feelings toward the brand? What are the ingredients to brand desire, and how does a brand manager learn to build great brands? There are many measures to assess brand desire:

It's my favorite brand.

I would pay more money for this brand than for other brand choices.

It is the only brand for me.

I am definitely going to buy that brand next.

I trust this brand.

As easy as it is to ask these types of elements as agree-or-disagree rating scales in consumer market research, they do not explain why people feel a certain way. These statements are synonyms for brand equity. They do not describe why people feel this way, for example, toward Duracell batteries versus Radio Shack branded batteries.

Several years ago, Ipsos followed a path to learn about the drivers and components of this brand desire (brand equity). Based upon tens of thousands of individual consumer brand assessments, we arrived at our brand equity model about what drives brand health (the in-market competitiveness of the brand loyalty). This is our model, as determined by empirical data through partial least squares modeling. This is not a theoretical model, but one based on factual consumer data. It is called Equity*Builder (see Figure 12.1).

**Fig. 12.1** Equity*Builder Model for Brand Health

The greater the brand achievements (on the left of the Equity*Builder) for the components or ingredients, the greater the brand performance on the right. Brand managers can specifically drive these components of brand health. How do they do this? The answer is that brand managers have a set of tools to affect their brands. They manage the "Ps" of their brand:

Product performance (product choice for retailers)

Package performance

Package artwork

Promotional efforts (advertising, coupons, sales)

Public Relations

Price

People buzz (word of mouth)

Place (store distribution characteristics)

Personnel (retail service)

And perhaps other Ps

So how does a brand manager best drive the success of his or her brand? The following pages share many of the lessons extracted from the Ipsos databases.

# C H A P T E R

**13**

# 35 LESSONS LEARNED

**LET'S LOOK AT THE TOOLS OF THE BRAND MANAGER (THE Ps) AND THE** components of Brand Health. What have we learned? What is important? What are the best practices?

## 1. FAMILIARITY IS KEY: YOU CANNOT LOVE SOMETHING YOU DO NOT KNOW

In order for a consumer to consider a brand and to have a favorable attitude toward that brand, it is important to build brand beliefs. This is more than just brand awareness ("Oh, I have heard of that brand"). Often brand managers think in terms of building awareness of new products as a key step to getting interest and a trial, *but brand awareness alone, without building brand understanding and brand beliefs, is not useful.*

We saw in Part 1 that decision making is built on assessing current attitudes and beliefs and having expectations related to each decision. So it makes sense that if we don't have favorable beliefs and expectations in our

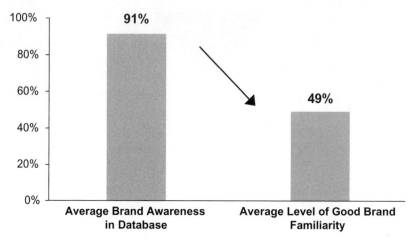

**Fig. 13.1** Difference between Aided Brand Awareness versus Brand Familiarity

*Source:* Ipsos-ASI Equity*Builder database.

head, then it is hard to arrive at a positive future brand decision. In our Ipsos research, we observe many consumers who have heard of a brand but who lack an understanding of it. Often a lack of positive beliefs leads to negative attitudes, and over time the brand becomes perceived by consumers as being unique and inappropriate. As a result, they lock this brand out from their consideration set. In a sense, the brand falls on the wrong side of their habits, their desire for consistency, and their risk-aversive brains (see Figure 13.1).

When building a new brand or new benefit, it appears to be useful to build familiarity or understanding and to choose the right advertising media and messaging that will allow for an education regarding what to think about the brand. Big brands can often afford large advertising campaigns that can effectively reach 90 percent or more of their target audience. If a company cannot afford a high level of reach to their target with informative messaging, it is preferable to restrict the reach to ensure that those who are reached get a good brand or understanding, even if it means achieving lower brand awareness among the total target in favor of greater understanding. Why? Because the knowledge leads to better motivation among those who are aware and it leaves the unaware as a pure opportunity in the future. *To create high brand awareness without good brand understanding can often work against the brand,* as the consumer puts the brand on the outside of his or her consideration set. Once consumers are sensitized to a stimulus and process it, the brain then works to desensitize itself to the stimulus. It is better to build familiarity than have a consumer desensitized to a brand before he or she has built positive emotional associations with the stimulus or memory.

## 2. BEING DIFFERENT OFFERS A COMPETITIVE REASON TO BE CHOSEN

We stated earlier that humans are wired to detect irregular things. We are less likely to focus on things that blend in or are familiar. Predators look for weak vulnerable prey, and fruit gatherers look for healthy fruit. These traits have existed for millions of years; they were present in our ancestors, and through evolution they are present in us. These are survival skills, and they have not evolved out of our genes in the recent centuries of living in a more developed world.

The implication for brand management is that it's better to stick out from the norm and give the consumer something to consider. However, marketers have to be careful, because although we see greater purchase loyalty for brands with unique features or differentiation, brands lose their loyalty if they become too different. The graph illustrating statement 2 (Figure 13.2) shows that brands with little uniqueness earn low purchase loyalty, and then as uniqueness ratings increase for various brands, we see higher loyalty, but only up to a point. Once a brand becomes very unique, it tends to become less relevant and less mainstream.

An explanation for this caution lies in the type of brands that become very unique. Often unique brands become niched or special occasion brands. For example, Stella Artois beer is considered unique compared to other mainstream beer brands in North America. Budweiser, Miller, and Coors brands are felt to be more mainstream compared to Stella Artois. So what happens? Consumers who choose Stella Artois do so on special occasions, perhaps as a treat, or when out on an important date, or with a client upon whom they wish to make a favorable impression . But then, for mainstream purposes such as having a beer with friends (at the barbecue or picnic, at the sports stadium, and so on) these beer drinkers are more likely to drink mainstream brands such as Budweiser, Miller, or Coors. These occasions are not so appropriate for the uniqueness of Stella Artois. In turn, Stella Artois is

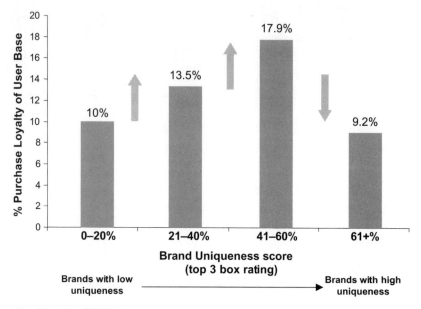

**Fig. 13.2** Purchase Loyalty versus Uniqueness
*Source:* Ipsos-ASI Equity*Builder database.

consumed occasionally and earns low share of consumption. Many drinkers of Stella Artois also drink mainstream brands.

This business model might be attractive to Stella Artois (as a niche brand). If they wish to grow their business and improve their brand loyalty, they likely need to be perceived as less unique and make their brand appear to be more relevant on more occasions. It is a challenge to make a unique niche brand more relevant without losing its uniqueness.

## 3. BE UNDERSTOOD FOR YOUR RELEVANCE

Motivation is largely dominated by the concept of hedonism (the gimmes). That is, people do things that are in their own self-interest, things that bring them positive feelings or reduce negative feelings. Almost every decision we make is a consideration of how to improve our feelings and satiate our desires. In terms of motivation, the promise of the brand needs to be positive and appropriate to the person. If the person does not find a stimulus,

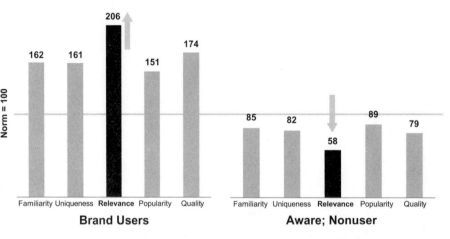

**Fig. 13.3** Components of Equity (Equity*Builder)—Index Scores
*Source:* Ipsos-ASI Equity*Builder database.

event, or decision to be appropriate for him or her, then it will not have as much attractiveness as it otherwise could have. So relevance is key.

In our equity model, the relevance measure has the strongest contribution to driving the desire for brand choice and has a strong correlation with purchase loyalty.

Correlation of Relevance to Purchase Loyalty = 0.68

The biggest difference between being a brand user and not being a brand user is this perception of brand relevance. In the graph illustrating statement 3 (Figure 13.3), we see that the brand users (in the left) score brand relevance higher than the other components of equity, while the nonusers (on the right) score relevance the lowest of the five components. Relevance is the biggest difference between users and nonusers.

## 4. THE QUALITY OF THE BRAND PROMISE AND CONSISTENCY, OVER TIME, DRIVE DESIRE

I doubt many will be surprised at the idea that consumers prefer higher quality performance to lower quality (all else being equal). Of course, when we consider price, consumers may choose to compromise on quality to afford a

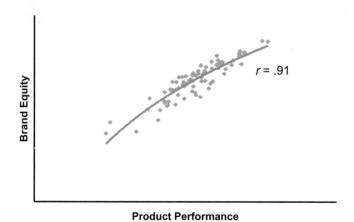

**Fig. 13.4** Brand Equity x Product Performance (Brands)
*Source:* Ipsos-ASI Equity*Builder database.

lower price, but this changes the subject to value (the combination of quality and price). We will talk about this shortly when we review price and value.

For service providers (banks, airlines, hotels, restaurants, retailers), the consistency of the quality performance is key. Consider flying: when a trip goes well, it is what we expect. Five good trips with one airline can be easily nullified by one bad experience. It is important to have consistency so that we can have fair, accurate expectations for our decision making. Expectations are a core element behind one's ability to make a purchase decision. Our expectations need consistency, and if we experience problems one out of five times, then the one failure will become part of the decision process.

In terms of the many tools (or Ps) available to the brand manager, the strongest influence on brand equity is product performance. Performance drives model measures of relevance and of quality and, in turn, drives overall brand equity. The graph representing statement 4 (Figure 13.4) shows the strong, direct relationship between brand performance and brand equity.

Although many people in the advertising business believe that the domain of brand equity rests in advertising, it is *product performance* that is the number one driver of brand equity. This shouldn't be a surprise to anyone because, as consumers ourselves, we would not buy a product a second time if we were unhappy with the product's performance (no matter how many ads we see for the brand). Manufacturers and service providers need to do everything they creatively can to deliver strong, consistent product performance. As competitors copy the performance of a brand, the solution is to innovate with new performance benefits. This is often more effective than advertising, but needs to be put into perspective.

## 5. ADVERTISING CAN MAKE A SIGNIFICANT DIFFERENCE WHEN PRODUCT PERFORMANCE IS SIMILAR BETWEEN COMPETITIVE CHOICES

Although product performance is a key driver of brand equity, many of the leading brands in each business sector or category are similar in their product performance. How much meaningful difference do you feel there is between the product performance (ignoring the branding, equity, artwork, and so on) of the top brands of bottled water, colas, batteries, pain relievers, food wraps, garbage bags, bar soaps, banks, hardware stores, dry cleaners, car rental companies, or appliance manufacturers? Many of the lower-priced discount brands or private-label retailer brands perform well enough to be considered for purchase. In a proprietary Ipsos survey, we asked consumers how they would rate the lower-priced brands in terms of absolute perfor-

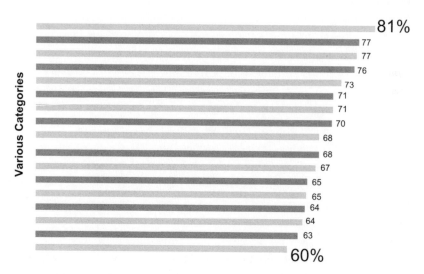

**Fig. 13.5** Store Brands Perform "Well" or "Very Well" (% agreement by category)
*Source:* Ipsos-ASI Equity*Builder database.

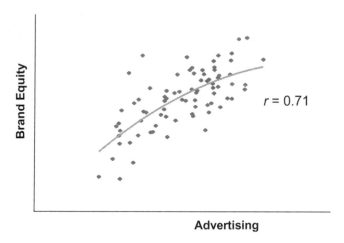

$r = 0.71$

Advertising

**Fig. 13.6** Brand Equity x Advertising (Memorable + Impactful)
*Source:* Ipsos-ASI Equity*Builder database.

mance: very good, good enough, or not so good. Many lower-price brands are scored high on overall product performance (see Figure 13.5).

However, product performance is not the only criteria for choosing a brand. In addition to product performance correlating with brand equity, we find in our data that good advertising also correlates with consumer brand equity; memorable, appealing advertising can also enhance brand equity (see Figure 13.6). This is an example of emoti-suasion by building extra, intangible elements onto a brand (beyond raw product performance).

There is much more to advertising than this implies. If we recognize that product performance is important, what happens to the importance of advertising when two competitive brands have similar performance? Advertising drives better brand equity when product performance is similar. In the following example (Figure 13.7), I picked pairs of brands (within the United States) with similar product performance ratings (two low scoring brands, two medium scoring brands, and two high scoring brands). The brands with the more favorable advertising recall also achieve higher brand equity (and we know through our Equity*Builder model that better equity leads to better in-market performance). *This is the key insight: when product performance is similar between competitive brands, there is an opportunity to build emotional associations through advertising. This is where advertising plays its biggest role, making similar brands unique.*

|  | Product Performance (1–10 scale) | Advertising (1–6 scale) | Equity*Builder (Index to 100) |
|---|---|---|---|
| **Category: *Orange Juice*** | | | |
| Sunny Delight | 6.08 | **3.81** | **119** |
| Floridagold | 6.34 | 3.28 | 74 |
| **Category: *Pain Relievers*** | | | |
| Tylenol | 7.41 | **4.16** | **177** |
| Advil | 7.45 | 3.99 | 149 |
| **Category: *Salty Snacks*** | | | |
| Doritos | 7.95 | **3.86** | **161** |
| Lays | 7.90 | 3.75 | 151 |

**Fig. 13.7** Better Ad Recall Boosts Better Brand Equity
*Source:* Ipsos-ASI Equity*Builder database.

|  | Average Scores from Ad Test Cells | Control Cells (Norm = 100) | Gain from Ad Exposure |
|---|---|---|---|
| Overall Equity Index | **130** | **100** | **+30** |
| ***Equity Components*** | | | |
| **Familiarity** | 141 | 100 | +41 |
| Relevance | 109 | 100 | +9 |
| **Uniqueness** | 143 | 100 | +43 |
| Quality | 114 | 100 | +14 |
| Popularity | 115 | 100 | +15 |

**Fig. 13.8** Impact of TV Ads on Components of Equity (Equity*Builder)
*Source:* Ipsos-ASI Next*TV database.

We also understand how this advertising works by reviewing the components of brand equity. Of the five key equity components in our model, our pretest database (Next*) shows advertising's greatest impact is driving *familiarity* and *uniqueness* (see Figure 13.8).

Advertising does not have much of an impact on changing perceptions of quality or relevance. These two dimensions are better driven by product performance. Consumers are proving not to be so naïve! We do not score a brand as good quality and appropriate just because the ad tells us so. We judge the product performance and find that the proverbial proof is in the pudding (not in the advertising).

## 6. TRIGGERING IS OFTEN THE BEST OBJECTIVE FOR ESTABLISHED BRANDS

Brand managers and advertisers should keep in mind the capability of advertising to boost familiarity and to help differentiate the brand. If neither is required for the brand (or not possible), then reconsider the purpose of the advertising. If consumers are fully familiar with a brand, perhaps the advertising function should be focused on brand triggers. It is not enough to have attitudes and beliefs in consumers' heads; they must also be triggered at the appropriate occasion. Thus, for many mature, established brands, the role of advertising is to trigger the desired associations already in the minds of consumers (who will desensitize to the familiar).

We can also see the contribution of advertising to brand equity by exploring differences by heavily advertised markets (such as the United States) versus lesser markets (such as French speakers in Quebec). In regions where advertising is more plentiful, we see a greater contribution of advertising onto equity. In Quebec, where there is less advertising for all the branded products, we see that advertising plays a lesser role than in the United States.

## 7. POPULARITY: SECURITY IN NUMBERS

In his book *Influence: The Psychology of Persuasion* (1984), Robert Cialdini talks about the power of "Social Proof" to influence consumers. The idea here is that by observing other people doing something or by knowing that others are also buying a certain product creates positive psychological factors influencing us to do the same thing. Cialdini calls this *social proof*. In our equity model, we believe this is the explanation behind our measure for popularity. We discovered in our data and in our model that by including a measure of brand popularity, we could make our model tighter (explain more variance); we were not quite sure why; it was just a factual observation. I often explained this as security in numbers, but I was happy to see Robert Cialdini's separate approach to this concept.

This seems to relate to our genetic evolution as social beings. By virtue of being social, we have lived along with others in our communities. For the vast majority of our time (98 percent of the history of mankind), we were hunter-gatherers. By observing other community members, we learned what was safe to eat and what was not (which mushrooms were good and which ones made people sick). This observation was a survival skill and allowed those with the skills to live to pass on these genes to the next generation. Thus, we appear to have a genetic evolutionary benefit to observe and do what others do (unless, of course, it leads to disaster). There is security in numbers. Marketers should consider this in their sales efforts (e.g., use of testimonials from common shoppers, quoting the numbers of current customers, or by referencing popularity, such as "author of the best-selling book").

## 8. EMOTIONS ADD AN EXTRA DIMENSION BEYOND THE RATIONAL ELEMENTS OF PRODUCT FEATURES

From our research tools and in discussions with advertisers, we refer to emotional response as the first emotional reaction to a stimulus (an ad, a taste of a product, a smell of a fragrance). This emotional response is automatic, unavoidable, and a genetic evolutionary outcome of how our nervous system works. The implication of this emotional response is that it leads to different possible sets of behaviors. A positive emotional response (like the fragrance of a new laundry detergent) is more likely to lead to positive behavioral outcome (buy the brand of detergent), compared with a negative emotional response (dislike the scent of a new detergent), which is likely to lead to no sales behavior.

So how do we measure this emotional response? Since humans show their emotions through facial expressions and body language, it is logical to use human figures to illustrate the different emotions. Showing our emotions has been a form of human communication through much of our evolution. It is genetic and appropriate for all cultures because all humans share the same emotional demonstrativeness. Conversely, emotion-laden pictures of calm lakes, beautiful flowers, or threatening scenes are not universally perceived for their emotional meaning; a scene of a calm lake might be relaxing to one person but boring to another. Humans are not skilled at interpreting the many subtle differences and nuances of emotions in others, either; thus, we felt it was better to use drawings to dramatize the more subtle emotions. Through much R&D and consumer testing, we arrived at our Emoti*Scape tool for use in our research with consumers.

In the Ipsos consumer research studies, we show this map of emotions (Emoti*Scape) to respondents and ask them to indicate the location on the Emoti*Scape that best represents their feelings (for example, emotional response to an ad or to a brand). The following Emoti*Scape (Figure 13.9) presents the answers from many different respondents' evaluating an ad. Each dot represents a respondent's emotional feeling, and the square represents the average or centroid of all the answers.

The responses of thousands of consumers across hundreds of studies evaluating different ads or brands are then added to the database. From this Emoti*Scape database, built up over time, we have observed a direct pattern between the consumers' emotional response and their purchase interest.

The Emoti*Scape shown with dots (Figure 13.10) shows the overall pattern across hundreds of studies. This relates the purchase intent toward a brand and the consumer's emotions to the advertising for the brand. Dot 1 on the Emoti*Scape represents the average or centroid of all the answers from the respondents who said they would definitely not buy the brand. Dots 2, 3, 4, and 5 show the progression for the average of emotions from other groups of respondents, building up to the top group (dot 5), who definitely intend to buy the brand. There is a clear progression; the more actively positive consumers feel in their response, the more interested they are in buying the brand. This provides the license to believe that the Emoti*Scape and that emotions themselves matter. Respondents' answers (charted on the Emoti*Scape in Figure 13.10) offer us insights into how a test ad is achieving or failing to achieve success.

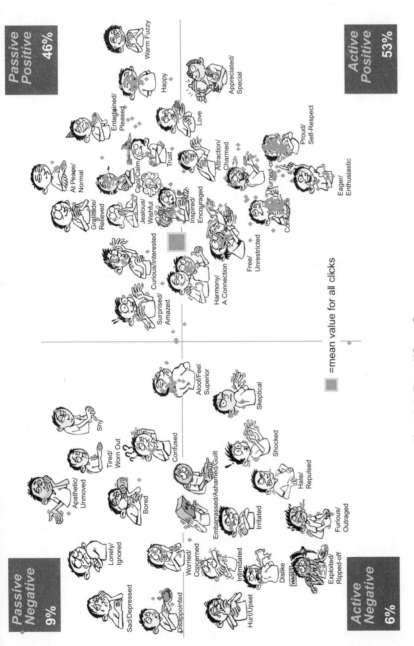

**Fig. 13.9** Emoti*Scape©

*Source:* Property of Ipsos. Copyright protected.

**Fig. 13.10** "Emotions toward Ad" x Purchase Intent
*Source:* Property of Ipsos. Copyright protected.

But emotional response is only the starting point for motivation and behavior. Advertising, as well as all of marketing, can create emotional responses, but the soul of marketing, and particularly advertising, is to motivate and to persuade, not just to create emotional responses. As we discussed in the first part of this book, emotions are only one step in the bigger process of understanding motivation and behavior. It is important to look beyond emotional response to understand behavior. Everything and anything creates an emotional response. As discussed in the chapter on senses, every stimulus causes an emotional evaluation in our brain. We have an emotional response to the ceiling over our head, to the most recent meal we ate, and so on. It is not only soft, emotional stimuli (advertising with babies, soothing music, or emotional imagery) that create an emotional response. For example, an advertising campaign that announces in black letters on a white screen that all Porsches will be half price next month would likely create quite an emotional response in many people, despite the lack of emotional creative.

## 9. ADVERTISING'S ROLE IS TO BUILD EMOTIONAL ASSOCIATIONS FOR THE BRAND'S BENEFIT

The primary objective of advertising is not to create an emotional response to the ad, but is *to create emotional associations onto the brand itself.* Ads are fleeting, as they come and go in a matter of seconds, but it is the brand that exists, and it is the brand or service that we pay for. The role of advertising is to create emotional associations for the brand, and over time, to trigger these emotional associations in the right motivational manner. We can help ourselves by referring to ads with terms other than "emotional" versus "rational." The reference to emotional advertising implies using soft imagery within the advertising rather than putting emphasis on the brand effect. We need to recognize that overly emotional, soft advertising can lack persuasive power. Upon further exploration of emotional responses to advertising using our Emoti*Scape, we observed the importance of engaging consumers (rather than just creating positive feelings).

We observed that persuasive ads attracted many emotional responses

**Fig. 13.11** Curious/Interested

in the upper right quadrant of the Emoti*Scape (Passive-Positive). We also observed higher emotions in the bottom right quadrant (Active-Positive), but most ads do not drive consumers to feel so excited and keen. We typically do not get more than 25 percent of responses in the bottom right quadrant.

With so many responses in the upper right quadrant (Passive-Positive), we felt it worthwhile to review each icon (we call him "Emo," and "Emma" for a female Emoti*Scape). To our surprise, the biggest difference between persuasive ads and nonpersuasive ads was observed for the Curious/Interested Emo (closer to the middle), and not the Happy or Warm/Fuzzy icons on the far positive right (see Figure 13.11).

Persuasive ads = 31 percent of respondents click Curious/Interested

Nonpersuasive ads = just 13 percent click this Emo

Meanwhile, the "Warm/Fuzzy" and "Happy" Emos (on the extreme right positive side of the Emoti*Scape) get little differentiation between persuasive and nonpersuasive ads. Thus, it's not so desirable to make an ad that obtains high positive emotional responses if it fails to engage the consumer to create intrigue, curiosity, and interest. We have such emotional ads in our database that have failed to be persuasive. There are exceptions, but risk management is about betting on the odds. The real point is that the advertising has to build emotional associations *toward the brand.* The ad has to create curiosity and interest to the brand. Such engaging ads outperform overly emotional, mushy ads. It is less important for the ad to be emotional just for the sake of emotion.

## 10. IT IS IMPORTANT TO GO BEYOND EMOTIONAL RESPONSE TO SELF-PERCEPTIONS, ASPIRATIONS, AND COMFORT ZONES

Just because a consumer feels curious or appreciated does not fully explain his or her behavior: is the consumer curious and wanting to try the product because life is short and it's fun to try new things, or is the consumer equally curious but unlikely to buy the product because he or she is risk averse? As covered earlier, emotional response only starts us in one direction or another. As we have learned, other things, such as self-perceptions, cognitive styles, and expectations, also affect motivation and behavior.

In our interview module of questions for consumers, we start with the Emoti*Scape questions (for the initial emotional response), but we then move to the next question, which is about personality associations. After conducting our research, we settled on 11 factors to describe personal elements for a brand along the lines of cognitive styles like the Myers Briggs test. Here, we ask respondents to tell us how well each of the 11 personal factors are associated with using the brand. Do they perceive brand use as being outgoing/extraverted/social, as emotional/touching/sensitive/feeling, or as selfless/giving? We cover 11 different factors and allow clients to add their own factors if they wish. We show the results on a web chart to compare, for example, how two different brands may be perceived, or to compare how a new ad compares to a control sample that have never seen the test ads. The web plots the average score for each of the 11 attributes. In this example, we show the web from the control sample that scored the brand without seeing the test ad versus a group that scored the brand after seeing the test ad (see Figure 13.12).

Being fact-driven at Ipsos and wanting validation that our tools work, we often ask, so what? Across the thousands of individual respondent evaluations of ads and brands, we have learned that the more personal associations a brand has, the higher the purchase intent to buy these brands. In Figure 13.13, the right side shows the higher purchase intent for the brands with a greater number of personal value associations.

We thought that this might be biased by happy brand users, so we explored this pattern among just users of the various brands. We found the same pattern. The overall purchase intent scores are higher among brand users because these are repeat purchases, but the top answer—definitely will

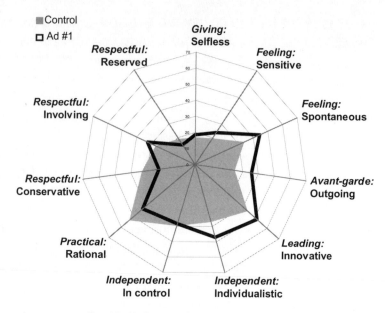

**Fig. 13.12** Personal Associations Web

*Source:* Ipsos-ASI Next*TV database.

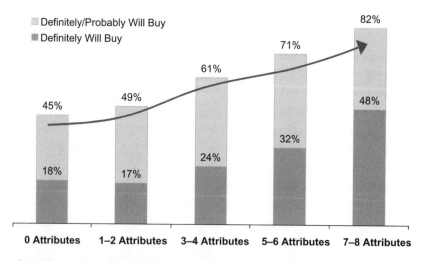

**Fig. 13.13** Purchase Interest by Total Number of Personal Associations Associated with Brand

*Source:* Ipsos-ASI R&D data.

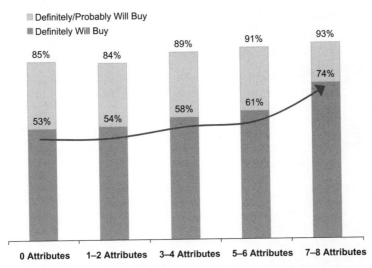

The greater the number of brand associations for personal associations,
the higher the purchase intent

**Fig. 13.14** Purchase Interest among Brand Users
*Source:* Ipsos-ASI R&D data.

buy this brand—is much stronger for the group on the right side, which has more personal associations for their brand (see Figure 13.14).

Not all brands can or should aspire to offer all personal associations. Brand managers need to conduct consumer research to understand which personal associations are associated with their brand, which ones are driving greater brand equity, which elements the competition own, and, overall, to consider how important emotional considerations are for the specific category (some categories follow a cognitive style that is more emotionally important than others). We observe that ads that can enhance one or more of these brand associations are more likely to be persuasive. Increasing consumer perceptions for these personal associations correlates positively with greater brand purchase interest (see Figure 13.15).

A central characteristic of self-perceptions is our personal satisfaction with how we are perceived. Often people aspire to be perceived in a better manner. Consumers can select brands that satiate their aspirations, as the brand's associations reflect the self-perceptions the consumer seeks. We explored this issue of aspirations in our equity R&D research. We asked respondents to evaluate their personal associations for the brands and then asked the respondents to evaluate themselves. If the brand was scored the

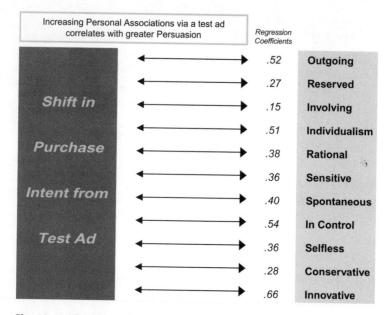

**Fig. 13.15** Correlation of Personal Associations with Ad Persuasion
*Source:* Ipsos-ASI Next*TV database.

same way as the respondents scored themselves, we refer to this as a match. This was done for all 11 personal associations in our surveys. We then asked respondents to tell us which elements they wished to have more of and which elements they wished to have less of. This latter approach was to determine peoples' aspirations and to assess how well the brand matches their aspirations (see Figure 13.16).

• • •

From our data, we observe two noteworthy patterns and correlations.

1. The closer the brand perception is to how the consumer perceives himself or herself, the higher the purchase interest for the brand. This pattern is evident for brand users as well. That is, consumers like to buy brands that share their own personal associations or perceptions (brands that fit their comfort zone).

2. There is also a higher purchase interest for brands that match consumers' aspirations. This relationship is weaker than the pattern for brands matching the consumers' comfort zone; consumers have a

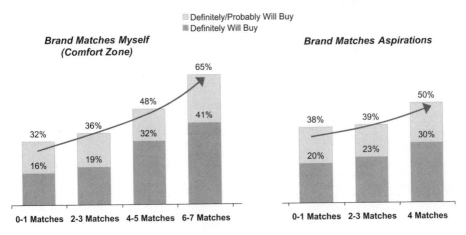

**Fig. 13.16** Personal Associations: Brand and the Consumer
*Source:* Ipsos-ASI R&D data.

greater intent to buy brands that match who they are than brands that represent their aspirations. Nonetheless, aspirations can help explain motivations.

Self-perceptions matter, just as psychologists theorize. We are more likely to buy brands that make a statement, that fit our comfort zone, or that represent our aspirations. *Marketers should consider these aspects of motivation beyond describing basic product features and product end-benefits.*

The vast majority of category users understand the big idea of the physical, rational characteristics of established products found in grocery stores and drug stores. They do not need to be continually told what they already know, so by doing so, advertisers are losing the opportunity to use their advertising dollars to better leverage motivational drivers such as emotional response and self-perceptions (to create emoti-suasion).

## 11. EMOTIONAL NEEDS, WANTS, AND DESIRES DRIVE OUR MOTIVATIONS

There is a third question in the emotional module in our surveys. Here we ask respondents which emotional needs they feel a brand satiates. We have 11 emotional drivers/needs (just like we have 11 factors for personal associations). These emotional drivers are factors that represent

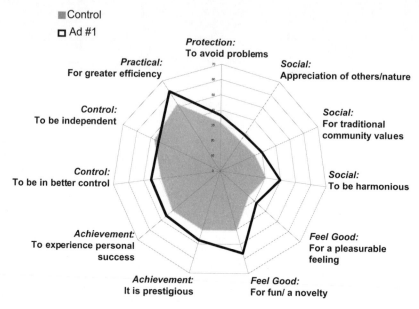

**Fig. 13.17** Emotional Drivers Web
*Source:* Ipsos-ASI Next*TV Database

needs, interests, drivers, wants, and so on, which all humans have across all regions of the world; we differ by how much of each we seek and by how we fill or satiate a given need, but these are basic core drivers. We asked respondents to consider each element and to indicate if they associate the driver with the brand or not, then sum up the scores to get a profile for each brand. The resulting graphic (Figure 13.17) shows the 11 factors in use in a web chart for the same brand; we see the web scored by respondents from the control cell and the other scored after seeing the test ad.

The purchase or use of a brand satiates one or more desires and provides emotional payoffs for us. Our desires are a consequence of being human. Emotional desires follow our hedonistic bias to make decisions that give feelings that are more positive or that avoid negative feelings. Again, we can ask, so what? The answer is that there is a relationship between these emotional drivers and purchase intent. The more emotional drivers associated with using a brand, the greater the desire to buy the brand. We observe the same among brand users for repeat purchase interest toward the brands. This is separate and beyond the physical, tangible characteristics of a product or

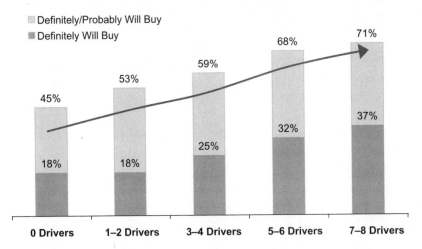

**Fig. 13.18** Purchase Interest by Total Number of Emotional Drivers Associated with Brand
*Source:* Ipsos-ASI R&D data.

service. The implication is that brand managers should consider emphasizing emotional drivers to better drive motivation (more than just talking about rational, tangible, known product features) see Figure 13.18.

How does this work? These 11 factors of emotional drivers are just a basic generalization. One can define more detailed, specific drivers and emotional desires. We encourage this and invite clients to add a few custom emotional drivers specific to their respective brand and category.

Some marketers have asked how is it possible that a brand can have several different emotional drivers or associations that almost appear to contradict each other. For example, how can someone say Starbucks is both outgoing/extroverted while also being reserved/quiet/introverted? The fact is that some successful brands score well on many emotional associations, and this likely explains why they are so big. A hugely successful brand needs to appeal to many people, addressing the majority of their desires or needs; otherwise, sales opportunities will be limited. By appealing to and offering many emotional payoffs, these big brands earn greater consumer support. Starbucks drinkers are happy to be seen with their Starbucks cups, and almost experience a showoff-type pride while walking around with their Starbucks coffee. One does not see nearly as much of this behavior with McDonald's or Dunkin Donuts coffee cups. In this manner, Starbucks has associations of extroversion, of individualism, of prestige ("look at what I have"). On the other hand, if you were to go to a retail coffee shop to have a quiet, harmoniously reserved experience, where would you go? Starbucks offers a nice environment that has soft, pleasing music with nice warm natural colors and subdued lighting. It is quite acceptable to sit by oneself for half an hour, drink a coffee, and watch the world go by—or a great place to meet a friend. Doing the same in McDonald's would not appeal to many of us! It is brighter, noisier, and less emotionally appealing. Thus, Starbucks also offers emotional associations that are reserved/introverted. In turn, whatever mood a coffee drinker is in on the introverted-extroverted spectrum, Starbucks can satisfy their emotional needs. Since McDonald's is weaker for both sets of emotional associations, it is not as likely to satiate a coffee drinker's mood (except perhaps, for a cheap, quick, convenient coffee purchase). Thus, Starbucks is appropriate for more emotional needs/occasions. In turn, they have grown rapidly into a large coffee retailer, and they are continuing to grow, offering a more expensive product.

This works in advertising. If one can improve the emotional associations with the brand (for personal associations or for emotional needs/drivers, or both), one can drive persuasion and increase purchase interest. Our ad-pretesting database supports boosting such emotional elements. We can explain about 50 percent of advertising persuasion by looking at improvements in emotional associations (via stepwise regression analyses between our Emo module and persuasion measures).

## 12. BRAND ICONS, CHARACTERS, AND SPOKESPERSONS STRENGTHEN BRAND EQUITY

Another benefit of advertising is that it can help create proprietary icons and characters (e.g., the Pillsbury Dough Boy, Tony the Tiger, the Energizer bunny). These icons can help improve the brand identification of a new ad and add more attraction to the brand, beyond its raw product performance. These extra icons or characters add personality, appeal, emotional elements, and extra tools for the marketers to leverage (another tool for emoti-suasion) that the lower-price brands and no-name products tend to lack. And the major brand icons are often protected by trademark laws. So do they help?

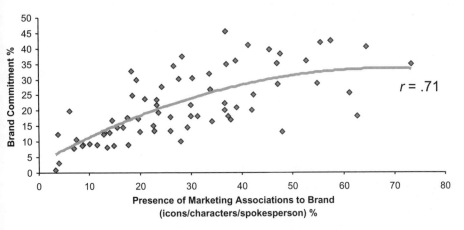

**Fig. 13.19** Brand Commitment by Marketing Associations
*Source:* Ipsos-ASI R&D data.

Yes, and likely in many more ways than simply driving recognition in ads or on the store shelf. These advertising icons help to drive increased brand equity because they contribute extra, unique elements for brands. In the United States, we assessed 75 different consumer brands across 15 different product categories and asked respondents if they associated a distinct character, icon, spokesperson, or unique advertising property with the brands, and if they felt positive, neutral, or negative toward these associations. We also asked our Ipsos Equity*Builder questions to quantify the brand equity for these same brands. In our analysis, we found a direct correlation between having a unique icon or character or ad property and stronger brand equity. In a sense, the icon or character represents an extra dimension to the brand purchase. The chart illustrating statement 12 (Figure 13.19) shows the strong relationship between commitment to the brand and the brand having such marketing associations (icons, characters, spokespersons).

## 13. APPEALING TO MANY DIFFERENT SENSES ENRICHES A BRAND

Earlier, we discussed how external stimuli enter our nervous system through our five senses and then fire unique neuronal patterns into various parts of our brain. The more different senses associated with a brand the greater the neuronal activity. In exchange, the brand should have a better potential for a rich burn-in that will build positive associations for it.

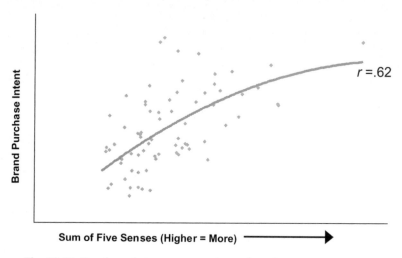

**Fig. 13.20** Purchase Interest versus Appealing Sense Associations
*Source:* Ipsos-ASI R&D data.

At Ipsos, we often refer to the five senses of the brand as the *brand physique*. This is the profile of the brand separate from its features, performance, and uses. For example, Perrier offers its sparkling mineral water in a unique green tear-shaped bottle. The packaging is not important in delivering the performance of the water, but it does offer a distinct look and feel to the brand. This brand physique can add extra sensual elements to an otherwise indistinguishable product. In a sense, this green bottle is part of what makes Perrier a brand. The physique of a brand can be important, and it can be used for a competitive advantage.

Earlier we reviewed some of the details of our study about brand physique and the five senses. We presented a graph showing a positive relationship between the quality or richness of the senses associated with brands and of consumers' purchase interest for them (Figure 13.20 is the same graph shared previously).

The implication is that creating and owning distinct sensual associations is helpful in making a brand more competitive. However, many brands do not do well in this regard. The absence of unique associations across the senses is not so damaging to a brand overall. But what happens when two products are similar? When competitive products are similar in features, price, and store distribution, any conceivable distinction for a brand is likely worth leveraging. We can see the benefits of this in a unique statistical analysis we use at Ipsos called penalty-reward analysis. This is a simple concept, although the math is not. The concept is that some brand attributes for a product or service are important as the price of market entry. That is, if the brand lacks a specific attribute, it's severely penalized. An example might be that the brand of car you buy must be safe. If the car lacks safety, you are unlikely to consider the brand—but, on the other hand, you are also unlikely to be excited by the safety of a car. Safety is a penalty attribute, not a delight attribute. The attributes that make the car appealing might be the legroom, the power of the engine, the soft, quiet ride, and the sound system—rewarding attributes that drive brand empathy. Typically, a brand has attributes that are necessary requirements but do not add delight, while having other attributes that are not so important but whose presence adds greater reward. It is useful to determine which attributes or associations are important as a penalty and which act as rewards.

When the penalty-reward analysis was conducted for the 75 brands in our specific brand physique study, we found that each sense acts more as a reward rather than as a penalty. The size of each bar in Figure 13.21 (determined by multivariate analysis) shows the proportional value as a penalty as well as a reward.

We conclude that the five senses can add to the purchase interest for a brand, but that the lack of a distinct sense (texture, look, scent, taste, sound) may not be so penalizing. As recognized in Chapters 1 and 2, brands are under attack, and a good way to manage a brand is to add unique emo-

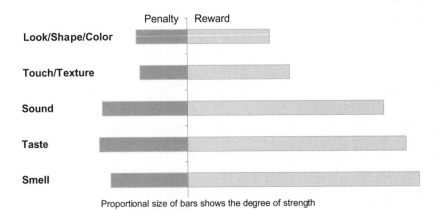

Proportional size of bars shows the degree of strength

**Fig. 13.21** Penalty-Reward for Senses (to Purchase Intent)
*Source:* Ipsos-ASI R&D data.

tional associations. Adding unique, appealing sensual associations is not only useful, but also perhaps necessary, even if adding such characteristics may add costs.

## 14. BEING EXPENSIVE IS ACCEPTABLE BECAUSE IT IS VALUE THAT MATTERS MOST

Why do people pay $500 for a bottle of Bordeaux wine? Part of the answer lies in the scarcity and exclusivity of the brand. In some cases, the more the price increases, the higher the demand. I believe it is easier to sell 50 milliliters of a nice perfume at $40 than to sell 500 milliliters for $4.99! These examples are extreme and do not apply to the mainstream. For the majority of products, we do not observe a strong relationship between price and desire for the brand (or between price and purchase loyalty). Figure 13.22 shows no strong relationship between the comparative price of brands and the purchase interest to buy the brand (the same relationship holds true for purchase behavior as well).

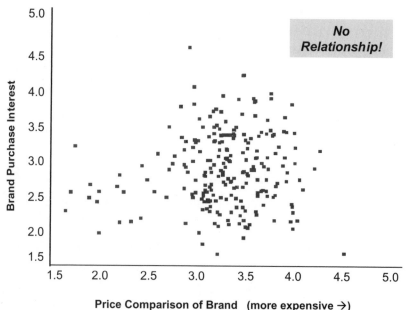

**Fig. 13.22** Purchase Interest versus Price Comparison
*Source:* Ipsos-ASI Equity*Builder database.

In many categories, the biggest, most successful brand is also one of the most expensive. Starbucks is an example of an expensive but successful growing business. So price is not as important as an isolated characteristic. It is *value* that matters. We define value as what you get for what you pay:

$$\frac{\text{What you get}}{\text{Price}} = \text{Value}$$

The denominator—price—is easy to understand, define, and measure. The numerator (what you get) is difficult to assess, because it means different things at different levels, and it includes both the rational tangible elements and the emotional (unconscious) intangible benefits. Thinking of high-end national (advertised) premium brands, the "what you get" is usually a combination of good product performance + attitudinal equity + emotional payoffs, but at the low-end, private-label price brands, what you get is mostly based on just-good-enough product performance (without much extra attitudinal equity). To address this, we have produced a value equation that combines product performance, brand equity, and price. We see that this modeled value score correlates well with in-market sales share (.90 correlation). It is acceptable to be expensive (and sometimes outright desirable) as long as we manage the value of the brand.

## 15. PRIVATE-LABEL RETAILER BRANDS AND DISCOUNT BRANDS ARE BECOMING GOOD ENOUGH AND ARE REDUCING THE RELEVANCE OF HIGHER-PRICED NATIONAL BRANDS

It is true that value is key (not just the price), but it's likely preferable (more profitable) to differentiate by competing on equity and emotions rather than price. However, there appears to be a threshold to the price consumers are willing to pay. Companies should avoid overengineering a product and having to charge a high price to cover the subsequent costs, as this may leave a large gap for a competitive product to enter at a lower price and with lesser features but still be good enough to compete.

As an example, consider disposable baby diapers from the leading manufacturers (Kimberly Clark's Huggies and Procter & Gamble's Pampers). Both of these diaper brands are super and can really absorb. They absorb about a pound or two of water, which is excessive, considering that most parents change their baby's diaper every couple of hours, after just a few bouts of urination consisting of a few ounces each time. These diapers, in a sense, are overengineered, so they compete mostly on secondary and tertiary features such as the closing tabs, the side-gathers, the clothlike feel, and the printed characters on the diapers. When modeling brand choice between these premium diapers, absorption is a small, unimportant criterion for brand choice, because all the major brands are very absorbent (so brand choice is based on other elements). These overengineered diapers are also felt to be expensive, creating an opportunity for big retailers like Wal-Mart or Costco to offer private-label diapers at lower prices. Admittedly, their products might be less well engineered, but they are good enough at keeping the baby dry for several hours.

In our equity database, we observe that there are now several categories that score well for offering lower-price brands that are good enough. As lower-price brands become good enough, they challenge and reduce the equity (+ relevance) of the higher-priced national brands. The challenge for marketers is to understand (track) the level of "good enough" and to be cautious of overengineering their products. The Average Relevance chart (Figure 13.23) from the Ipsos Equity*Builder database shows how brand equity is lower for brands in categories where the lower-price brands are good enough.

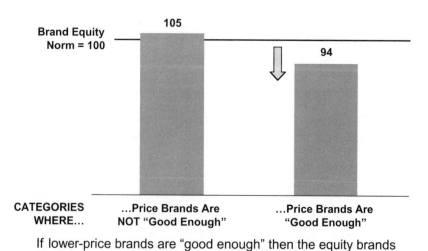

Fig. 13.23 Average Relevance Score of Brands from Various Categories
*Source:* Ipsos-ASI R&D data.

## 16. CREATIVE IS KING

I have been using this phrase for many years. (Unfortunately, I even used this expression when I was speaking at a conference in China. A colleague pointed out to me that perhaps I should consider a different approach for the communist Chinese culture). When it comes to the many elements of an ad campaign, more than 75 percent of the success of the campaign often hinges on the content and style of the ad itself. This should not be confused with the importance of product performance, which, as we saw, is even more important for sales success, but within the decisions about advertising and media planning, creative is king. Advertisers must air only strong ads to get their money's worth on their expensive media plans. I cannot overemphasize the importance of this.

In our advertising database, we looked at the range of in-market accomplishments for ad recall, across thousands of campaigns, all with about the same amount of media exposure (1,000 cumulative TRPs of exposure in North America). In the Range in Ad Recall chart (Figure 13.24), we can see a large range of difference at the same level of media exposure. Some

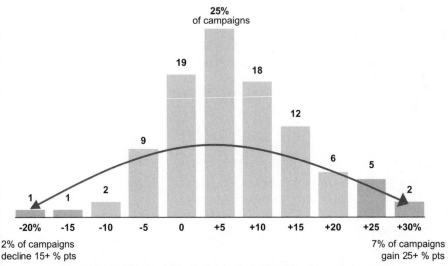

**Fig. 13.24** Range in Ad Recall (for the same cumulative media exposure of 1,000 TRPs)

*Source:* Ipsos-ASI Ad*Graph Tracking database.

campaigns have improved ad recall immensely (+30 percent point gains in ad recall), while others have allowed historic ad recall to decay (ending up with lower recall than at the start of the campaign: –20 percentage points). This illustrates the importance of good creative in driving success.

## 17. GOOD ADVERTISING GOES TO WORK QUICKLY

When the advertisement is good, it breaks through quickly and is recalled by consumers. On the other hand, if the creative is weak, it will not likely improve with more media exposure. It is also an expensive, high-risk business decision to keep spending money on media exposure behind a weak ad, hoping for an improvement. Consistent with other sources, within our ad tracking databases we observe that advertising builds in C-shaped convex-down curves; there is no wear-in (which would look like an S-shaped curve), and each additional exposure is less efficient than the one before. The Proven Recall graph (Figure 13.25) demonstrates how ad recall builds, split out by the top performing quarter of ad campaigns, and the second and third quartiles.

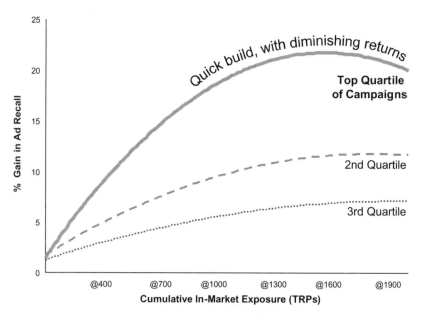

**Fig. 13.25** Build in Advertising over Time (Media Exposure)
*Source:* Ipsos-ASI Ad*Graph Tracking database.

This graph appears consistent with how we are genetically programmed to react to new stimuli and then start to desensitize to the presence of re-peated stimuli. I recognize that there is a difference between the advertising being recalled quickly versus the impact on the brand business. Although improving brand attitudes, or stimulating brand trial, or launching a new benefit may take time—and it may never happen—the advertising should be working right from the beginning. The advertising should be breaking through, be well branded, deliver its desired message or content, and be well perceived by consumers. If advertising for Kia cars was aired to convince consumers that Kia offers the highest-quality cars, then the advertising should get ad recall as it goes to air—but it could take years to convince consumers that Kia offered great-quality cars. Owing to the importance of creative, to be an efficient advertiser, it is prudent to conduct both ad pre-testing to allow only strong creative on-air and to do in-market ad tracking at an early stage so as to ensure that the creative is meeting its expectations. In advertising, we need to know which ads to air, and when to pull them off—like investing in shares on the stock market, one has to know both which stocks to buy, and when to sell them. It means knowing (quickly) when to withdraw bad advertising and knowing when good advertising is wearing out.

## 18. BAD ADVERTISING RARELY WEARS IN

Unfortunately, we have seen in our database many cases of advertising that have not performed well. Rarely does an ad campaign perform better over time (with more media exposure). Even if some could, would an advertiser want to pursue such inefficiency? The No Build in Recall graph (Figure 13.26) presents an example of weak advertising, over time, with a noteworthy amount of ongoing television exposure. Notice how frequency of exposure is not helping to build better ad recall. Consumers are desensitizing and tuning out. This is a typical pattern in our databases.

Making a television ad usually costs about 10 to 20 percent of the total ad campaign budget, with media costs representing the remaining 80+ percent of the budget. Ironically, the minor cost for the advertisement explains more than 75 percent of the effectiveness of the campaign. The other way to look at this is to appreciate that media exposure is expensive, and if you do not

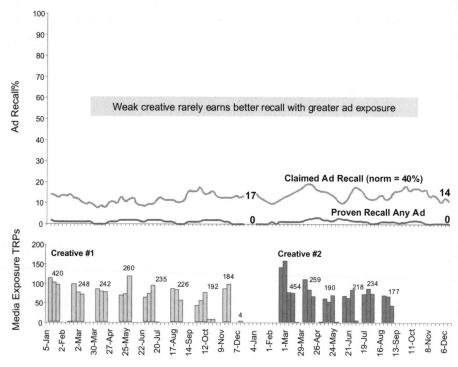

**Fig. 13.26** No Build in Advertising Recall with Weak Creative
*Source:* Ipsos-ASI Ad*Graph Tracking database.

have good creative, the media investment is not well leveraged. It is not a good decision to put a lot of media money behind a weak piece of creative in hopes that its high media exposure will compensate for the poor creative. The implication is that advertisers should pull poor performing creative off air quickly to avoid wasting more media dollars. Often it is a challenge to cut a new ad early because a lot of work has gone into making the ad, getting senior management approval, and paying for the production of the ad. As well, the media plan is often purchased well in advance and cannot be easily cancelled halfway through the campaign. In this case, I suggest replacing the poor ad with an older, proven, successful advertising (a good but worn-out ad is often much better than a weak current ad). Alternatively, give the media exposure to some other brand in the company portfolio. It is costly and inefficient to continue airing weak creative.

There is no formula for creating effective advertising, but there are general patterns and observations that can be leveraged to increase its odds. These patterns are found in the Ipsos databases, and they reflect how humans are wired. Effective ads are characterized by the following factors:

1. Interest value (to catch attention).

2. Relevant differentiation (to offer a meaningful reason to burn into our memory and consider the brand).

3. Simplicity of execution (so the brain can effectively file the memory and retrieve it later).

4. Branding properties (to ensure the brand is attributed to the memory unit).

The next several observations discuss these issues in greater depth.

## 19. MEMORABLE ADS HAVE SOMETHING THAT MAKES THEM STICK OUT

Advertising creative that is likeable, entertaining, unique, and engaging tends to earn greater ad breakthrough and memorable ad recall. This is consistent with our genetic tendencies to notice irregular stimuli, to engage the brain when it is exposed to something new, and to burn in enriched, engaging stimuli. Conversely, being safe, familiar, nondescript, and sticking with the status quo tends to go unnoticed. Our brains have a tendency to be lazy (energy efficient) and will not engage unless confronted to be engaged.

The Related Ad Recall chart (Figure 13.27) comes from the Ipsos database of pretested TV ads. Using the Next*TV tool, Ipsos uses a standard set of questions to ask respondents their attitudes and reactions to a television ad. A database is built across all the different tested ads. This allows us to learn what drives ad recall and persuasion. For ad recall, we have indexed the average amount of recall (within the database) to a value of 100. We see that ads with high likeability earn above-average ad recall, as do unique ads.

Norm = 100

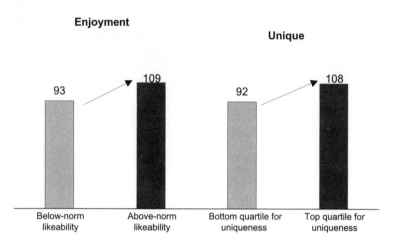

Fig. 13.27 Related Ad Recall in Next*TV Pretests

## 20. POOR BRANDING IS A MAJOR PROBLEM

When we talk about the creative being so important, we refer to the content, which includes the tone, style, message, production values, brand strategy, and so on. Among all of these characteristics, the most common failure we see in practice is the poor brand linkage of the ad to the brand. How often do you recall an ad (particularly on television, but also print ads, billboards, on the radio, etc.), for which you do not remember the brand in the advertising? This is one of the most noteworthy failures of advertising observed in our databases. Overall, about half of consumers who can recall a television ad when described to them (without using the brand name) cannot correctly attribute the advertising to the brand. Fortunately, advertisers can learn how to make better-branded advertising once they appreciate the nature of the problem and the need to make the brand an undeniable part of the ad memory.

## 21. KEEP IT SIMPLE—AND VISUAL

Since the brain is energy efficient (lazy) and humans do not deal well with complexity, it is logical to serve up advertising as an easy, simple unit. Al-

Norm = 100

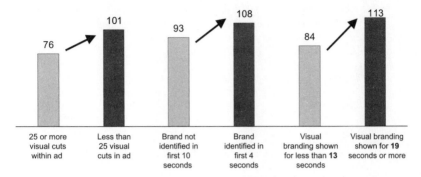

| 25 or more visual cuts within ad | Less than 25 visual cuts in ad | Brand not identified in first 10 seconds | Brand identified in first 4 seconds | Visual branding shown for less than 13 seconds | Visual branding shown for 19 seconds or more |

**Fig. 13.28** Related Ad Recall Norm in Next*TV Pretest

though this may sound dry, scientific, and formulaic, television ads tend to achieve better-branded recall when they mention the brand early in the ad, when they have a greater duration of brand exposure throughout the ad, and when they display the brand. Advertisements that have multiple scene cuts perform poorly, while simple and narrative storylines achieve better recall. We reviewed this earlier in the first section of the book when reviewing how the brain deals with memory. This is about avoiding complexity and recognizing that our brain works in discrete memory units, with a strong bias toward our visual sense. Naturally, there are exceptions, but our learning shows the benefit of getting the brand established. The Related Ad Recall Norm graph (Figure 13.28) illustrates the different characteristics and how they affect ad recall (from the Next*TV database).

## 22. BRANDING DEVICES ARE WORTHWHILE

Advertising campaigns that use icons, mnemonics, and unique ad properties tend to have better ad success. The assumption is that using such tools helps consumers to get the brand name as part of the ad memory. For example, when one sees the white tire character in an advertisement for car tires, there is little doubt that it is for Michelin tires (and it makes little sense for Goodyear, Bridgestone, and others).

Some advertising icons are undeniably linked to the brand (right from their first use) while others have become indirectly associated with the brand over time. Marketing campaigns that follow a similar consistent approach and

Norm = 100

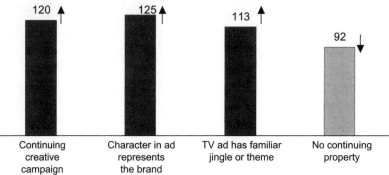

| Continuing creative campaign | Character in ad represents the brand | TV ad has familiar jingle or theme | No continuing property |

**Fig. 13.29** Related Ad Recall Norm in Next*TV Pretests

work to build and then leverage a campaignable ad property tend to perform better. At first, a specific model or actress may not be obviously and undeniably linked to Cover Girl or to L'Oreal, but over time, and with consistent use, the advertising can build this association (repeating it for the brain) such that by seeing the famous face, consumers correctly link the ad message to the correct brand. Ads that leverage past campaign properties in new ads or leverage brand characters or both tend to earn above average ad recall (see Figure 13.29).

Campaigns with undeniable brand linkage are those that directly leverage unique aspects of the brand name, the package, logo, or product. For example, Absolut vodka uses creative advertising that leverages their unique bottle shape. Snuggle fabric softener uses a teddy bear as the main character in their ads, which is the same teddy bear shown on the package. Consumers can see the ad and go to the store to buy the correct product without ever having to note the brand name. It's the one with the bear. This approach really came to life for me when a cereal client hired us to conduct consumer research, using Cantonese, among the many new Hong Kong and Chinese immigrants coming to Canada. We pilot-tested the survey and quickly learned that many Chinese immigrants were describing the cereal brands not by the brand name, but by their logos (the man with the black hat = Quaker Oats, the rooster = Kellogg's Corn Flakes). The picture was more meaningful to them than the brand name, and it was these pictorial elements that burned best into their brains. This is the normal visual tendency of the human brain.

Some icons that lead to good brand recognition include:

Tony the Tiger (Kellogg's Frosted Flakes)

Ronald McDonald (an undeniable linkage)

Michelin man (Michelin tires)

Colonel Sanders (an undeniable link to KFC)

Pink battery bunny (Energizer batteries)

Mr. Clean (an undeniable linkage)

Doughboy (Pillsbury)


## 23. MAINTAIN CONSISTENCY OVER TIME (BE CAMPAIGNABLE), BUT MAKE NEW MESSAGES OBVIOUS

This idea of consistency over time is to allow consumers to learn the branded icons or properties and then to leverage them in future ads so as to avoid the risk of future branding problems. Consumers learn and identify a brand's advertising properties over time. We come to recognize the spokespeople, the iconic characters, and the unique themes. This makes life much simpler and allows the ad to be processed easily and well in our memories. In turn, it makes sense for advertisers to leverage these campaignable properties when creating the next new ad for the brand. Consistently using the same ad properties helps to reinforce previous learning as well as enhance the correct future brand attribution.

However, as one continues to leverage past historic ad properties in new advertising in the future, it is also important to make sure the new executions are quite fresh and distinct. The problem is that familiar campaigns can become less engaging over time, as humans start to desensitize to what is already familiar stimuli, but since continuity and consistency offer other important benefits, it is worthwhile following campaignable initiatives. *The trick is to make sure that each new ad leverages the consistency, while also being new, unique, and fresh enough to be worthy of attention.*

This challenge manifests itself most obviously when an established campaign has become known for endorsing a specific brand message, but the advertiser wishes to introduce a new and different message. It is imperative that the new ad is perceived as being consistent with past ads (to leverage their benefits), but also it must be uniquely different—otherwise, consumers may easily relate this ad with the past messages without noticing there is a new message. We have seen many long-running, successful campaigns struggle to get a new message across.

Some readers may feel that a new strategic message requires a new creative campaign approach. This might be the case, but not only does a new campaign start from scratch, with all its risks of failure, it also runs the risk of creating cognitive dissonance among consumers (versus their past beliefs). It is likely better to evolve . . .

## 24. EVOLUTION, NOT REVOLUTION

Think evolution, not revolution. We have seen two truths in this:

1. Evolving and adding new considerations for a brand forces the consumer to engage his or her brand (process the new stimuli and consider it). We react more strongly to new, different stimuli. So keep evolving.

2. In general, new marketing programs are more efficacious if they evolve forward with direct reflections and appreciation of current brand properties without being too revolutionary. Marketing programs that are much different from consumers' current understanding of the brand are more apt to fail. Consumers do not work hard to see, hear, internalize, and think about each of the hundreds of advertising stimuli they are exposed to daily. Thus, if a brand team needs to follow a new marketing program in the future, the change needs to be made easy for consumers to appreciate. The marketing needs to recognize consumers' current impressions rather than to suddenly pretend that the current situation is over and now it is time to add a new, different brand proposition. Consumers may have cognitive dissonance, a disconnect between what they know and what they are now seeing. Consumers will be saying to themselves that this new brand proposition can't be for Brand X because I know Brand X, and this new thing isn't the same, so it must be for Brand

Y or Brand Z! We have seen many new marketing programs suffer from this cognitive dissonance and end up with brand link failure, doubt, confusion, and denial.

An example of evolution, not revolution is from the AVIS car rental company for their "Trying Harder" campaign. When this new marketing program started, they could have claimed, "We are new and improved. We are great." Instead, they recognized that for the consumer, Avis had room to improve, and that they were now following a path to be better. This program recognized that their brand was in position A and they were moving from position A to position B. This is quite different from suddenly announcing the brand is in position B, when consumers feel it is in position A. This "Trying Harder" approach is credible and is less likely to create a cognitive dissonance for what consumers currently knew of Avis at the time.

New marketing efforts need to help evolve and bring along the consumer into the future.

## 25. AIM FOR RELEVANT DIFFERENTIATION

It is important to recognize that many of the elements that make ads stick out and make them memorable and engaging may not be helpful for being persuasive and selling the brand. It is true that some elements that drive ad recall may also be the same reasons an ad is persuasive, and vice versa, but not always. Often ads fail to build sales because too much focus is put on breakthrough and recall. In turn, the ad fails to focus on the brand message. For example, humor can help an ad gain attention, and so can

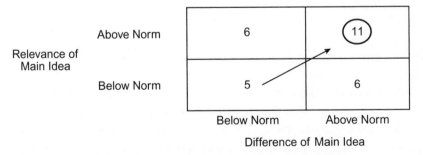

**Fig. 13.30** Average Brand Persuasion Selector Score

Norm = 100

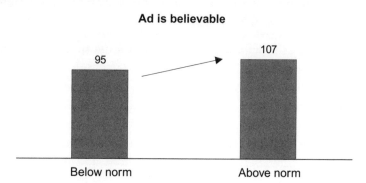

Fig. 13.31 Persuasion Index in Next*TV Pretests

celebrities, but these elements can upstage the brand and lead to a lack of focus on the brand sell.

We find in our Ipsos data that persuasive ads tend to provide a believable, unique, and relevant reason to consider the brand. The relevance of the message is a personal, subjective evaluation by the consumer and can be about identifying with the characters, the situation, or associations with the brand—or both. When the main idea of the ad is both different and relevant, we observe even better persuasion (see Figure 13.30).

In addition to relevance and differentiation, it is important to have believable ads. The Persuasion Index graph (Figure 13.31) comes from the Next*TV database of pretested TV ads. This shows the Persuasion score for the ads (where the average score is 100). It is likely of no surprise that believable advertising is more persuasive than unbelievable advertising. Thus, persuasive ads are both relevant and believable.

## 26. SOCIAL PROOF AND "BECAUSE"

Robert Cialdini writes about the psychology of persuasion in his interesting book *Influence: The Physiology of Persuasion*. Three specific elements he addresses are the concepts of social proof, authority, and the power of "because." That is, humans respond better when the selling message appears to come from someone of authority (for example, an expert or doctor),

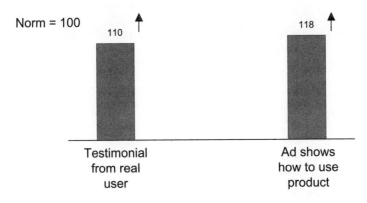

**Fig. 13.32** Persuasion Index in Next*TV Pretests

when we see or hear other consumers are also buying the brand, and when we are given a reason to believe the selling message. This latter concept is often referred to as the *license-to-believe* in many communication-briefing documents to the ad agency.

In our data, we see evidence of these elements. In particular, when testimonials are used in advertisements, from other users of the brand, we observe a higher persuasive effect than average. We also see that when an ad shows how to use the product we observe a higher persuasion effect than average. Again, advertising efficacy appears to be following the learning found in psychology and human sciences (see Figure 13.32).

## 27. ADVERTISE FOR A REASON: NEWS IS PERSUASIVE

Naturally, there are many reasons to advertise, and perhaps one of the common reasons is because the competition is advertising. Preferably there is real need, with real upside potential for the brand to advertise. Advertising just because the competition is doing so may not be sufficient justification or the wisest use of one's budget. A brand team needs to know how much of the brand's sales are in play as a function of advertising to justify advertising solely for defensive reasons.

A real opportunity for advertising appears when a brand has news, an innovation, new claims of use, or something to say that the consumer is not currently aware of. We observe in our data that ads that contain some

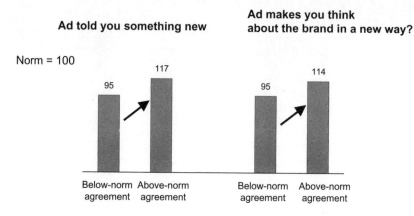

**Fig. 13.33** Persuasion Index in Next*TV Pretests

form of news for the viewer are more persuasive. Ads without news are not so persuasive (see Figure 13.33).

## 28. ONE UNIFIED CREATIVE APPROACH WORKS BEST

Sometimes we see a brand using different creative messages across various media. Perhaps there are good reasons for this, but this likely adds complexity for consumers. It fragments the messaging (in a cluttered media and busy advertised world) and dilutes the budgets behind each multiple message.

Within our databases, we observe that marketing campaigns that follow one unified, creative approach across their ads and media tend to perform better than campaigns that are more fragmented with different creative approaches in each media. Perhaps a unified creative approach keeps the message simpler and easier to internalize, with a more concentrated focus: "All for one and one for all." Our brains like to judge, classify, and file evaluations in simple summary units. The brand and its advertising should aim for one unified mental unit. The Ad Recall + Impact chart (Figure 13.34) comes from our Ad*Graph (in-market) tracking database.

It is also worth recognizing that as many advertisers explore the new emerging media channels (Internet, podcasting, video-on-demand, product placements, etc.), it is important to use these tools for their unique benefits. There are modern war cries in the advertising world these days: "integrated marketing communication," "total communications planning,"

■ Prompted ad awareness

▨ Increased interest (a lot/little)

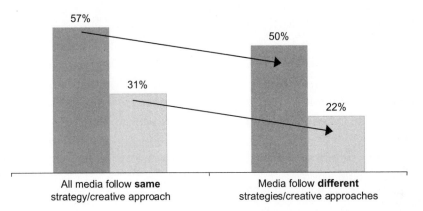

**Fig. 13.34** Ad Recall + Impact by Campaign Approach
*Source:* Ipsos-ASI Ad*Graph Tracking database.

"holistic marketing." As the media choices fragment and expand, experts now recognize the need to manage all the touchpoints together (including PR, blogs, sponsorships, word-of-mouth, buzz marketing, etc.). But this should not be confused with thinking "all the same, and the same for all." Our data suggests that campaigns that adopt a common, unified look or creative approach tend to do better—but surely, each marketing tool and media channel needs to be used for the distinct purpose and strength it offers. For example, billboard advertising may offer good, affordable brand reminders, but billboards tend to be poor for communicating detailed messages. Magazine ads are often good for communicating details, but they are expensive and may have limited reach in a short period. Radio advertising is more affordable than television, but television allows one to visualize the brand message better. Advertising can inform, but often promotions, home sampling, and in-store samples generate better trial. We have to consider the strategic needs for the brand, the marketing objectives, and how each media channel plays its role. So the concept is to leverage one common creative platform (to help our brains), but to use different marketing tools for different purposes.

## 29. ONE AD AT A TIME

We observe that television campaigns that air one commercial at a time tend to perform better than television campaigns that use several ads in a group or in a pool. That is, if one can afford to air more than one television ad in a year (or for many advertisers in the United States, per quarter or month), it is likely better to schedule them sequentially, airing the first one until it has worn out, and then moving to the second, third, and so on. Airing multiple ads at the same time likely adds complexity, fragments the effort, and dilutes the media exposure per ad. Thus, instead of having to process one ad with 100 percent of media support, the consumer is suppose to process *several* different ads, each with less than 50 percent support (this is complexity).

Sometimes I get the sense from advertisers that more is better. I can appreciate that more might be better than less, but this does not account for efficiency. More is not necessarily more efficient or a better use of limited resources. To make several ads in a campaign costs more money than the cost of one. So the payoff needs to be even higher for a pool of ads

**Percentage Point Gain in *Proven Ad Recall* @ 1,000 TRPs**

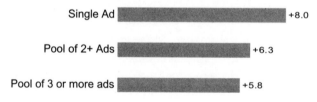

**Percentage Point Gain in *Brand Purchase Intent* @ 1,000 TRPs**

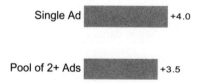

**Fig. 13.35** Percentage Point Gain in *Proven Ad Recall* and *Brand Purchase Intent* @ 1,000 TRPs
*Source:* Ipsos-ASI Ad*Graph Tracking database.

than airing just one advertisement. This is demonstrated by our in-market tracking database (see Figure 13.35).

Both ad recall and purchase interest are stronger for a single ad than for a pool of ads (at the same level of media exposure). It appears that a concentrated, focused approach is better than a diluted, multimessage approach. The former seems to fit better with our simple, lazy brains, while the latter approach adds complexity.

## 30. WEAR-OUT—IT HAPPENS

We join the chorus of supporters that sing, "Long-term success is largely a collection of short-term successes." Few campaigns fail in the short term but work in the long term. Few ads will wear in. The decisions are uncomfortable but relatively obvious: quickly pull bad ads off air. But what about the successful piece of creative? When does the short-term success end, calling for a replacement ad?

We define *wear-out* slightly different from others. An ad has worn out when it is no longer the best use of your next advertising dollar. This happens before the ad stops working. This definition of wear-out reflects the point of inefficiency. Consider the Pony Express, used when the U.S. postal service would send mail with riders on horseback. As they raced westward, the most efficient (quickest) way to get the mail to the west was to replace the horse with a fresh one when the rider's horse was tired, not dead. That is, the initial horse might still be able to carry on, but if it is just plodding along in an exhausted state it is not efficient. There is a point when it is better to get on a new, fresh horse before the first horse tires. In terms of replacing television advertising, we refer to this point of efficiency as the time of commercial wear-out. In our Ad*Graph tracking databases, this appears at about 1,000 to 1,300 cumulative TRPs of exposure (in general). And this relationship seems to hold up in all markets (because a unit of exposure means the same thing in each market) with little variation for the advertising environment or culture (perhaps ±10 percent), and little variation between new and mature brands (see Figure 13.36).

By switching to a new ad, the advertiser brings a new stimulus to the consumer. This forces the brain to evaluate this stimulus and to process it. New stimuli get more attention than old, familiar, already-processed stimuli.

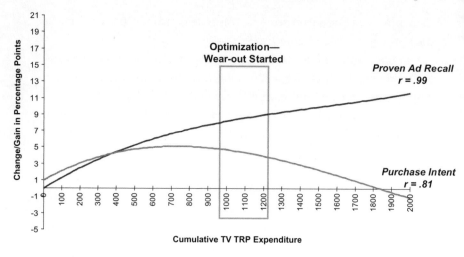

**Fig. 13.36** Ad Recall and Purchase over Time (Media Exposure)
*Source:* Ipsos-ASI Ad\*Graph Tracking database.

In practice, if one had enough money to afford 2,500 cumulative television TRPs for one piece of creative, it would often be more cost-effective to make a second ad and only afford, say, 2,200 cumulative television TRPs (using the cost of 300 TRPs to make the second ad). You would wish to air one ad for the first 1,300–1,400 cumulative TRPs, and then air the second, fresh (pool-out) ad for the remaining 800–900 TRPs. At the end of your budget, you will likely have achieved more (despite a few hundred TRPs less of media exposure). This is what we learn from in-market tracking. This is optimizing the efficiency of the advertising budget.

## 31. BETTER MEDIA PLANNING CAN PAY OFF

The media plan (schedule, budget, and execution) is often the least exciting part of the advertising function for marketers. It is more challenging, fun, and important to develop the ad. However, the media plan likely costs 85 percent of the advertising budget, and if one can improve the media plan 15 to 20 percent, there is a noteworthy dollar benefit. Personally, I feel many marketing professionals do not understand this costly side of the business well enough. It is time for a paradigm shift in media planning. A shift away from quantitative measures of cost-per-point, reach, frequency, and absolute dollar allocations per media. I am not talking about the next wave of technology. I refer to the concept of planning media schedules on quality measures and efficacy as a reflection of consumers getting it and responding.

We all likely know that one set of 100 TRPs (for example, 50 Reach × 2 Frequency) is not necessarily the same as another set of 100 TRPs (25 Reach × 4 Frequency) even if the cost is the same. But Ipsos ASI has also proved that one TRP is not the same as another because of the difference in quality of the exposure. The likelihood of paying attention to an ad exposure in one showing on Monday morning is different from the attention spent (quality of exposure) toward a different exposure some other time. Thus, the question: would you pay a 10 percent premium for an ad exposure if it achieved 20 percent better attention from consumers? The answer is likely yes, but many media plans and media optimizer models are based on optimizing costs and costs per point (or cost per 1,000 viewers) without a concern for the quality of the exposures. The new evolution in digital entertainment presents an opportunity, almost a necessity, to create more efficacious media schedules based on quality characteristics.

Discriminating variables for predicting better viewing behavior during commercial breaks include:

- Enjoyment of the show (which may be different from the prime-time hit shows)

- Frequency of watching the same show

- Day part; time slot and day of the week

- Program type

- Seen program before (rerun)

- If ad break is within the show

- Location of the TV in the house

- If viewing alone or with others

These differ by key demographics.

How do we know this? We conducted a consumer survey using telephone interviewing. Since we doubted people could remember what they watched or did last evening, we felt the only reliable recall of television viewing attention would be for the previous 15 minutes. Thus, we conducted each interview *minutes* after each commercial break, while the viewer could still accurately remember what he or she was doing minutes prior. We randomly telephoned adults, across the whole day, every day of the week, for 10 weeks. We only included adults who had the television turned on when we called. We then asked about the television program and the last commercial break just minutes before. In the interview, we asked consumers which ads they could recall, how much attention they felt they paid to the ads, and which of several activities they did during the ad break (including switching channels, doing other activities in the room, leaving the room, and watching any of the ads). We also asked about the viewer's show enjoyment, frequency of viewing the show, and so on. After each interview, we coded the show type, channel, and recorded the time and day of the week.

In general, attention to advertising is not so high! I do not intend to degrade television as an advertising medium because I am sure attention levels for each magazine ad, newspaper ad, billboard, and web banner is also low. We found that some situations earn better viewer attention for television ads than others and that viewing behavior is not well predicted by surrogate (people meter) surfing data. Surfers do not have lower ad attention levels, and surfing is likely better than if the viewer temporarily leaves the room or is totally ignoring the television. Therefore, it is worth determining which situations offer better viewing and to then plan media buying around these qualitative measures of efficacy. We have identified several measures that can help achieve more effective media buys.

I recognize that this study was just about television, but I strongly suspect that the same considerations apply to each of the other advertising media. That is, there is much more to consider when determining the efficacy and best practices of a medium than the costs. Some billboards are easier to see than others are, and we react differently to Internet ads and pop-ups by the time of day. I have read about the nature of magazine ads working differently based on which magazine that ad is seen in. One study I recall referred to an ad for a dress. When consumers were asked their opinion of the price for the advertised dress, their answers differed as a function of the different magazines in which the ad appeared. The context of the magazine content affected the perceptions of the ad. If this context effect is more than 5 to 10 percent, then surely (owing to the significant amounts of money spent toward advertising) advertisers should demand more effective media planning approaches. The industry needs a paradigm shift toward efficacy and the quality of media exposures, but this must come from the manufacturers and service providers, since it is these firms that have the money (not the ad agencies, nor the research firms).

With the appreciation that each TRP (unit of exposure) is not equally effective, we can now build on this to consider the cumulative level of media exposures. The Ipsos ad tracking databases show strong evidence about cumulative media exposure over time. Some of these follow in the next pages.

## 32. SHARE OF VOICE IS LESS IMPORTANT THAN MOST MARKETERS THINK

I sense that there is a feeling of security in bombarding consumers with the same message to ensure they get it. This is kind of like the desire to shout at others when we get mad or anxious. Although share of voice correlates positively with advertising success, it is less important than other elements, and aiming for high share of voice is a costly proposition. This begs the question about efficacy and best use of money.

As we reviewed earlier, creative is king. Making and airing only good, fresh ads is far more important than achieving high share of voice. There is lots of proof for this. One can simply verify this by adding all of the media exposure in a given category (for example, all television advertising campaigns for all brands of breakfast cereal for six months), and then review the ad success and impact for each brand. We often find that brand achievements are based on the strength of their creative (more so than the strength of the share of voice).

Please don't get me wrong. Share of voice does correlate positively, all things being equal, but it is not as important as other things. The concern should be in answering, "What is the best use of the budget?"

## 33. RECENCY PLANNING IS EFFECTIVE

John P. Jones addressed this concept in his 1995 book *When Ads Work*. We also observe the benefits of recency planning in our databases. Jones offers solid evidence that the closer (more recent) the brand's ad exposure is before the category purchase, then the more likely the ad is to drive sales of the brand. The concept, then, for recency planning is to plan an advertising exposure to each consumer as close to their purchase occasion as possible. Naturally, this is hard to execute, as we do not really know when each brand purchase will happen, but if sales are happening each week, and each month, then it stands to reason that one needs constant advertising exposure such that there is never a dark, off-air period when several weeks could go buy without an ad exposure. Since one might not be able to afford continuous advertising at a meaningful level, we see that a blinking strategy, use of shorter TV ads (15 seconds), and use of alternate media can be effective. If you are off-air, and the competition is reaching your target, then the recency of exposure will benefit the competition.

The following chart (Figure 13.37) refers to ad recall as a function of heavier pulsed media flights versus a more continuous recency plan. This is from the Ipsos Ad*Graph media model based on thousands of tracked television campaigns. Both plans include the same cumulative level of TRPs and for the same number of weeks. However, it is the recency plan that provides more people with recall across the period. It is not an issue of how much share of voice one has when on-air. It is about good creative, spread out over time. This Modeled Proven Ad Recall chart shows how two equal media plans can create different levels of Ad Recall depending on how the media schedule is planned. The media plans that are more continuous typically work more efficiently.

Part of the explanation behind this observation is that advertising builds with diminishing returns. That is, as one tries to drive up ad recall, it will grow as a C-shaped convex-down curve, leveling off as it gains. Thus, it is hard to increase ad recall unusually quickly as a function of spending lots of money. Conversely, when advertising stops, ad recall decays. The off-air periods are not neutral. They are detrimental. Media planning should concern itself with both aspects: build and decay. I appreciate that this is not a new concept, but often I sense that advertisers are trying to maximize the build (to obtain the biggest impact on the upside) instead of minimizing the decay. *Much of the Ipsos evidence suggests that marketers should be more concerned with minimizing the decay.* Trying to maximize the build, through high share of voice, is costly and it fights against diminishing returns. On the other hand, recency planning works. It helps to prevent the

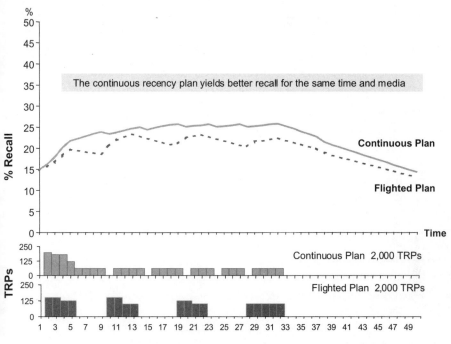

**Fig. 13.37** Modeled Proven Ad Recall (Ad*Graph Media Model)
*Source:* Ipsos-ASI Ad*Graph Tracking database.

decay. And avoiding overexpenditures is a more efficient use of funds. It may not be so attractive or aggressive, but minimizing the decay is an efficient way to approach advertising budgets. This allows one to consider the use of multiple (different) media in a cost-effective mix so as to constantly get in front of consumers. This leads to the next media issue.

## 34. REACH IS THE KEY ELEMENT AFTER CREATIVE

The idea behind recency planning is to reach all category buyers each week, or every second week if one cannot afford every week, or once a month if this is what is affordable. The main word here is *reach*. It is not as useful to reach someone two or three times this month, if it means using money that is now spent and not available for next month. It is better to see an ad once a month (each month), than to see three ads this month and nothing for the next several months. This latter approach of seeking frequency today instead of reach tomorrow is the opposite of recency planning, and it proves to be less effective.

The one main exception would be for the introduction of a new initiative. Our data support the benefit of a short, focused burst at the beginning of a new campaign, to get it on consumers' radar screens and then quickly focus on coverage (recency plan) across the rest of the budget period. The previous chart in the discussion of recency planning shows this initial burst at work.

We see the role of reach when we observe how consumers internalize ad recall for a new initiative. Ad recall builds in a similar pattern to the build in reach of the campaign to consumers. Ad recall does not build in the same pattern as cumulative frequency of exposure to the ad. The ad recall curve in our Ipsos Ad*Graph database levels off, as does the media reach curve (while the cumulative frequency curve keeps building; see Figure 13.38).

After achieving high reach among the target consumers, the goal is to reach them all a second time, and third time, and so on—but do not reach some consumers a third or fourth time if you have not reached everyone a first or second time. The concept is to create unduplicated reach cycles. A cycle has been completed each time 85 to 95 percent of the target has been reached. Advertisers should plan to conduct as many unduplicated

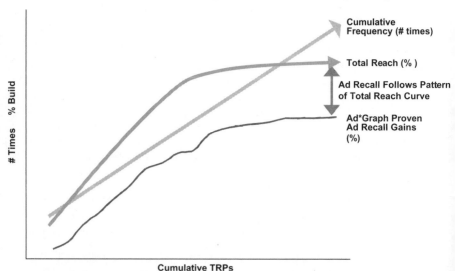

**Fig. 13.38** Build in Advertising over Time (Media Exposure)
*Source:* Ipsos-ASI Ad*Graph Tracking database.

reach cycles (everyone once, then everyone a second time, etc.) as they can afford. A large brewery or car company can likely afford to conduct a reach cycle every couple of days, or at least once a week, whereas a small brand may only be able to afford a reach cycle once a quarter.

In practice, it is hard to avoid hitting the couch potato several times before reaching the infrequent television viewer once, but this is the goal. The plan is to aim to optimally maximize reach and reach cycles, while reducing excessive frequency. This can be pursued with confidence if one understands that share of voice is not a good measure to maximize. And even if the cost per TRP increases by attempting a high-reach media buy, the efficacy and value might likely be better than a cheaper high-frequency media buy.

## 35. MEDIA CONSUMPTION DOES NOT MATCH WITH AD RECALL

As media planners start to consider the concepts of reach and recency planning, while also keeping in mind the quality of each ad exposure, we should point out that advertising recall does not follow the patterns of media consumption as measured by conventional audience measurement tools. In North America (and perhaps it is similar elsewhere), the consumption of television increases with age. Older viewers consume several more hours of television per week. However, older consumers generally have lower ad recall. Internalized ad recall is much higher among teens and gradually decreases across the older age groups. Thus, how advertising works is different from how consumers consume the media. Media planners and advertisers need to keep this in mind, because planning media based just on audience ratings per program is inconsistent with how advertising works. Teenagers do not need more or greater ad efforts just because the audience measurement indicates they consume less TV. Our data shows they have about double the internalized ad recall of older adults! The Television Ad Recall chart (Figure 13.39) shows Ad Recall Norms by different age groups. Notice how younger respondents have higher recall, even though, on average, they consume less television per week.

I believe that younger adults and teenagers have a greater interest and social need to be aware of the latest trends. They have greater social pressures

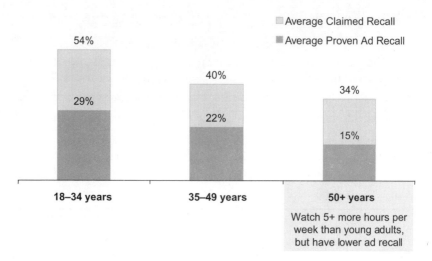

**Fig. 13.39** TV Ad Recall by Age Group
*Source:* Ipsos-ASI Ad*Graph Tracking database.

to fit in and to be in the know. Conversely, the average 55-year-old male is less likely to be trendy and less fussy about defining his world by advertising. In addition, perhaps advertising creative is not well understood and produced for the average 55-year-old. They may have grey hair, but their attitude may be 20 years younger. They may need Attends soon, but they will be wearing them while driving around in some new sports car. I am not sure why older adults have lower ad recall despite consuming more media, but this is the reality. I hope it's not because their brain cells are slowing down!

• • •

To end Part 2, let's revisit the beginning: much advertising underperforms and is wasteful. Marketing managers need to manage the odds of advertising success by better managing the process, by focusing on efficacy, by measuring and leveraging the science of advertising. Marketers can learn from the genetic nature of mankind. It has taken me many years to learn all of this. I hope you can benefit more quickly and put some of this to work for your business. This is not the end of the learning, just the end of this section of the book! We all need to keep following the science, with a focus on efficiency. Our learning should never stop.

## PART 2 TAKE-AWAY: SUMMARY OF KEY LEARNING

• Manage the odds. Build a better process. Pretest and track marketing programs. If you do not measure marketing, it is hard to manage it.

## KEY LEARNING

1. Familiarity is key: You cannot love something you do not know.

2. Being different offers a competitive reason to be chosen.

3. Be understood for your relevance.

4. The quality of the brand promise and consistency, over time, drive desire.

5. Advertising can make a significant difference when product performance is similar between competitive choices.

6. Triggering is often the best objective for established brands.

7. Popularity: security in numbers.

8. Emotions add an extra dimension beyond the rational elements of product features.

9. Advertising's role is to build emotional associations for the brand's benefit.

10. It is important to go beyond emotional response to self-perceptions, aspirations, and comfort zones.

11. Emotional needs, wants, and desires drive our motivations.

12. Brand icons, characters, and spokespersons strengthen brand equity.

13. Appealing to many different senses enriches a brand.

14. Being expensive is acceptable because it is value that matters most.

15. Private-label retailer and discount brands are becoming good enough and are reducing the relevance of higher-priced national brands.

16. Creative is king.

17. Good advertising goes to work quickly.

18. Bad advertising rarely wears in.

19. Memorable ads have something that makes them stick out.

20. Poor branding is a major problem.

21. Keep it simple—and visual.

22. Branding devices are worthwhile.

23. Maintain consistency over time (be campaignable), but make new messages obvious.

24. Evolution, not revolution.

25. Aim for relevant differentiation.

26. Social proof and "because."

27. Advertise for a reason: News is persuasive.

28. One unified creative approach works best.

29. One ad a time.

30. Wear-out—it happens.

31. Better media planning can pay off.

32. Share of voice is less important than most marketers think.

33. Recency planning is effective.

34. Reach is the key element after creative.

35. Media consumption does not match with ad recall.

CHAPTER

14

# CLOSING THOUGHTS

*Advertising people who ignore research are as danger-*
*ous as generals who ignore decodes of enemy signals.*
—DAVID OGILVY, ad agency executive

**IT MAY BE UNAPPEALING TO SOME TO FOLLOW MARKET RESEARCH AND TO** study the science of advertising, and it may lead to conflicts (as has been said before—the definition of conflict is when theory meets reality). If you do not measure it, you can't manage it. There is much learning to be had, and those who ignore it are more likely to repeat their mistakes of the past. Yes, a few can occasionally have success based on luck, but in the long term, the odds will catch up to most of us. Thus, it is likely best to manage the odds by using research, following a better process, and following the lessons offered by Ipsos.

In Chapters 1 and 2, we covered the challenges to modern brand management. The purpose of Chapters 3 to 11 was to explore how humans tick. Part 2 of the book then showed many lessons learned from the Ipsos databases. The sum is this: the best practices of advertising, marketing, and personal motivation follow the genetic evolutionary traits of mankind. This is the science of marketing. By studying how humans tick, we can learn how to be better persuaders, marketers, and advertisers.

## EVOLUTION AT WORK: A CASE IN POINT

I came across an interesting study that acts as just one example of our genetic evolution at play. Brunel University issued a press release (Sept 1, 2005) with the title "Survival of the Fittest: Women Win the Hunter/Gatherer Shopping War." This study analyzed the shopping habits of men and woman across 14 countries. It concluded that our genetic evolutionary traits continue to influence our current shopping practices today. Historically, for millions of years, men were the hunters, while women were the gatherers and managers of the camp and resources. These roles have endured for over 98 percent of mankind's existence. In turn, these roles have affected our genes and our nature. Today, a man is more likely to enter a store in a decisive, focused, and determined manner, as if he is on the hunt. Men are more likely to be focused on finding the right item (size, color, etc.), buy it, and leave. They have a purpose much like going on the hunt. And the shopping experience is not well liked (perhaps because working a kill is dangerous, tiring, and tough work). On the other hand, females approach shopping in a pattern consistent with their evolutionary traits as gatherers/managers. Women peruse, take their time, collect various different products, socialize, find the best value, and may even bring home more products than intended. Women find shopping a satisfying activity and they tend to achieve, on average, a 10 percent lower price than men.

Smart retailers take advantage of these evolutionary genetic gender differences. They lay out their products differently for men than for women. Male-oriented products are more likely to be concentrated in groupings so they can be easily found and compared. Female items are more scattered throughout the store, encouraging and rewarding the wandering and gathering nature of their genetic inheritance. This is just one example of appreciating the evolutionary nature of our genes and leveraging them for marketing that is more effective.

## BRAND MANAGEMENT IS ABOUT MANAGING
## TO THE EMOTIONAL GIMMES

Marketing is not about products and prices. It is about people and their lives. Product management is about managing the product; the performance, the physical features, the ingredients, and the costs of manufacturing or servicing, but brand management is based on the concepts of emotional associations, brand attitudes, imagery, persona, artwork, naming, and so on. These elements build the brand beyond the otherwise generic state of the naked product.

Effective brand management starts with good product performance. We learned that the product itself accounts for much of the brand's equity, and we discussed that some brands have great equity without much advertising. Starbucks is an example of this. However, good brand management builds on the foundation of good product performance to differentiate the brand and to leverage extra consumer appeal to justify a premium price, with less vulnerability to competitive activity. This is what is required today to compete against the damaging brand trends reviewed in Chapter 1. Brand management must more fully leverage the emotional payoffs and emotional gimmes that humans judge and seek: what are the emotional associations, extra senses, advertising properties, brand icons or characters, and emotional payoffs to consumers in their terms? Why should the consumer care or get excited about choosing one brand over another? This is appealing to the self-centered hedonistic core of humans. This is how we tick. This is the basis of emoti-suasion. In my opinion, this is what successful brand management will need to evolve toward.

I have been asked if emoti-suasion works for business-to-business marketing, selling to doctors, appealing to politicians, and so on. The answer is yes—because emotions and satiating personal (selfish) desires are genetically based in all of us, all of the time. For example, a pharmaceutical client was asking Ipsos about emoti-suasion as an approach to introducing their new prescription medication to health care professionals. The client had traditionally spent millions of dollars launching their brands by informing doctors of the benefits of their drugs, the side effects, drug interactions, and so on. This is all rational and mechanical and is similar to how other medications are often marketed to doctors. The shortcoming is that this approach misses the emoti-suasion and personal gimmes of the doctor. What are their emotional desires? Perhaps many doctors are motivated to build their professional reputation and may wish to be the first in their area to be prescribing the new medication. Alternatively, perhaps some doctors are risk averse and will only put their support behind a new medication once they have seen most other doctors prescribing it, too. Or maybe the doctor might wish to be perceived as being wise, so he or she chooses to reject the new medication based on his or her years of medical experience. These are the feelings and desires that many doctors consider (their personal self-perceptions) that directly affect their likelihood to prescribe a new medication. Pharmaceutical clients, like all business-to-business market-ers, have great opportunities to leverage emoti-suasion and appeal to the emotional desires/needs of their targets.

Emoti-suasion also applies to social marketing, politics, philanthropy, and environmentalism. As an example, one specific pet peeve of mine is the label "Global Warming." This term does not sound so emotionally bad, especially to those who live in cold-weather climates. It does not attack my emotional feelings and frankly, it has an appealing tone. It does not sound ominous for the dangers it causes. Instead, if we referred to the same problem with a more personally meaningful label (such as "global cancer generation," or "life-limiting destruction") then the problem starts to be more engaging and relevant to me, today. The emoti-suasion of such problems should be about the problems to me, to my health, to my existence, today. Jared Diamond writes in his book *Collapse* how the many empires, cultures, and societies that existed throughout history died away. One of the contributing causes to the decline of a society is mankind's short-term selfish nature. Our genetic nature leads us to care most about our self, today, and to care less for others sometime in the future. Thus, for an effective emoti-sausion, we need a new label to replace global warming, with a term that references our current danger, right now.

## IT IS NOT ABOUT EMOTIONAL ADVERTISING

This book required several chapters to describe how motivation is like a mul-tilegged stool. Marketing is not just about creating an emotional response. This is just the opening step. Many other characteristics come into play, such as attitudes, memory, self-perceptions, expectancy, triggering, and so on. Thus, the concept of emoti-suasion is the gestalt and the finish of all of this. Emotional response is the start, and the brand's emotional payoff is the end. This is important to recognize, because many advertisers are cur-rently focused on creating a positive emotional response within or toward the advertising. Consequently, they are not spending enough attention on the consumers' emotional gimmes. Yes, we may pay more attention when an ad creates a favorable emotional response, but we all know that the role of advertising is to persuade and sell, not just to entertain and create nice emotional responses. The focus needs to be on emoti-suasion (the benefit) rather than emotional response (the fleeting reaction to a stimulus).

For brand management, emoti-suasion is not about emotional, soft, mushy advertising, nor does it even need to include expensive advertising at all. Most advertising does not create much emotional response in us. We see this in the Ipsos ad-testing databases. Consumers would become emotionally unstable messes if we responded emotionally to each advertisement we see in our daily lives. But we are smart enough to understand the intent of most (good) advertisements, and this helps to paint the emotional associations onto the brand, either directly or peripherally. And it is the brand associations that are key, because humans change their moods, desires, and emotional needs from day to day and from week to week. Thus, it is hard to target and maintain the right emotional tone for the consumer. Advertising is mostly temporary and fleeting. It is the brand that is lasting and that consumers buy because of their emotional needs. Brands need to be the answer to these changing emotional needs. The more appropriate and more often a brand provides the desired emotional satiation, the more likely and more often it will be considered.

Painting the emotional gimmes for a brand can be achieved in many styles and approaches. To be clear, emoti-suasion can be achieved with rational, communicative hard-selling messaging. Conversely, often ads that are emotionally soft and moody fail to be persuasive because they do a poor job engaging the brain. They fail to credibly build the emotional associations onto the brand. This leads to an observation that I imagine most people appreciate: a brand is not cool or desirable because the advertising directly tells us so, but rather because we arrive at this feeling ourselves. Some brands fail by trying to directly tell consumers how to think or feel. This makes the message too public, too commercial, and causes us to question the seller's intent. One has to be cool by being cool rather than saying they are cool. Many of our emotional desires are subconscious and built on peripheral cues from the brand. Making the emotional payoffs so consciously obvious can lead to rejection.

## DIFFERENTIATION OR DOMINATION?

Often in the marketing industry, we hear that the role of marketing is to offer the brand with a USP, a *unique selling proposition*. That is, each brand needs to identify and stand for one clear promise. Although uniqueness may be an attractive feature to have, this concept is harder and harder to achieve, and perhaps is too narrow. What about the consumers' point of view? The USP represents the perspective of the brand owner in competition with other brand choices. For the consumer, the decision to buy one brand versus another is about what does it do for me, at the personal emotional level, with little regard for the brand managers' challenge. Consumers do not want just one benefit, but instead, they want many. For example, when purchasing a pain reliever, a consumer does not want to choose between the fastest acting brand, the safest brand, the longest lasting brand, or the least expensive brand. He or she wants all of these benefits, and more. Consumers also want the emotional payoffs (to get back into life, to accomplish goals, to avoid medicating my body, and so on). Thus, although having a unique product benefit might be useful for a brand manager, a consumercentric approach to brand management is likely better served by evolving the concept of the USP towards emoti-suasion in the consumers' perception.

Since emotions, personal values, and self-centered desires are the fundamental basis of our motivations, then it is likely important to recognize that consumers' purchases are not just based on product features (which are often similar between the leading brands). Many consumers buy brands because of their desire to fit in and harmonize. We see this in our Ipsos Equity*Builder database: popularity is a key ingredient in many brands' success, and we find in the Ipsos data that relevance is more important than being unique or different. The reason many consumers buy a brand is because the brand is not unique.

Perhaps the solution is to focus on the consumer and his or her emotional desires and worry less about brand characteristics and USPs. By adding self-rewarding payoffs for using the brand, one enhances the appeal of the brand. The broader and more all-encompassing the emotional appeal, the more often the brand will satiate the changing emotional needs of various consumers. In Ipsos brand data, we observe that 10 to 35 percent of the variance for explaining future purchase intent can be explained by the emotional associations of the brand, notwithstanding any consideration for pricing, product performance, packaging, distribution, and marketing program budgets. Successful brands—those with strong brand equity—appear to be able to offer many emotional associations and drivers. It is not about owning just one emotional driver, but offering many. *The more emotional payoffs the brand can provide, the more times the brand will be relevant to each consumer, whatever his or her desire or mood.* The optimal way for a brand to grow and to have a lot of appeal is to create and offer many emotional payoffs: to be all things to all people on a personal emotional level. This is not likely a surprise or contradictory. Consider the favorite people in your life versus those you just like. Do your favorite people offer you just one or two emotional benefits, or do they offer many different emotional payoffs across your many moods, situations, and desires? Favorite people offer many rich emotional payoffs. So should brands. Many of the emotionally charged brands have achieved this by avoiding a defining USP. Instead, these brands are positioned in rather vague ways, which allows each of us to create our own meaning for the brand. Nike simply says "Just Do It," Viagra simply shows happy people the morning after, iPod rarely uses words in its advertising, and Starbucks relies on personal experiences to build its brand equity. It appears that the big, successful emotional brands avoid narrow definitions of their brands to narrow target groups, based on narrowly defined media channels.

## SCREENING FOR BETTER ADS

For the readers who are true marketers and advertisers, I imagine much of your motivation for reading this book is to learn how to make better advertising. The good news is that advertisers can learn to make better-branded ads. It really starts with understanding how the brain works: we have lazy (energy-efficient) brains that prefer to work with simple, discrete mental units. The brain summarizes big ideas and dislikes cognitive dissonance. It responds to irregular stimuli and desensitizes to familiar ones. We like to form habits.

With this in mind, I suggest brand managers should ask themselves a few key questions that focus on the principal learning when presented with a new idea for an advertisement:

1. What is the creative Big Idea? (A two-sentence description you could give to a stranger.)

2. Is this a single, unified, simple Big Idea?

3. Is it strategically focused, and does it build emotional associations (payoffs)?

4. Does it undeniably involve the brand, with strong brand integration, for brand link?

5. Is it original, different, or novel to be irregular?

6. Is it campaignable (to build or leverage ad properties for future advertising)?

7. Does it leverage the power of because with a license to believe?

Each of these macroquestions reflects how our brains work and tries to evaluate advertising in a way that is going to make it easier to succeed. There are no promises with anything that includes an artistic element, and there are exceptions, but I always prefer to design things to succeed rather than to design for failure.

I also like to suggest that brand managers should receive and view the new proposed creative ideas *by themselves, as if they were the consumer.* Often, in my experience, the creative developers like to present the advertising idea by introducing the objectives and the background and describing how wonderful the final on-air ad will be ("We will book Nicole Kidman to star in the ad, get Steven Spielberg to produce it, and have the Rolling Stones produce the score!") This agency presentation distorts one's instinctive reaction, over-rationalizes it (too cognitive!), and it can be an intimidating situation for the brand manager. I have been there. Instead, marketing executives should evaluate the key questions on their own. View it the same way the public will be exposed, then review these questions free of external bias.

Occasionally an ad executive will ask, "Do you want us to make great creative, or do you want us to make ads that pass silly pretests?" First, these are not mutually exclusive goals, and second, if the ad passed our pretests, the chances of it succeeding have been improved immensely. Thus, my response would be both. Advertisers should give their ad agency a bonus for each ad test they pass. Passing a robust, validated pretest is good for sales. Rest assured, research tools do pass great (irrational) ads. Our Ipsos databases include many great ads.

Advertising needs to be treated as a business and as an investment, with all the discipline associated with risk management and leveraging knowledge. It may be nice to win a gold prize at the Cannes advertising awards, but this should not be the goal. Just like the big lotteries, someone will win the millions, but it would not be good financial planning to build a retirement plan contingent on winning the jackpot. It is smarter to understand, appreciate, and manage the odds

Please do not misunderstand me. I believe great creative is critical to advertising, but we can learn (along scientific principals and from databases) about how to make better advertising. Before making their masterpieces, most great artists learned from others (while many others have failed). Let the masses be the judge, since it is their opinion that counts most!

## ENOUGH SAID

Enough said. I have enjoyed the exercise of simplifying and clarifying my thoughts, beliefs, and experiences for this book. In turn, I hope readers have benefited enough to justify their personal investment in *Gimme!* I wish you good luck, and I thank you for your interest. This is the end, for now. I welcome any thoughts, questions, and comments. The challenge continues to evolve, and so must the learning.

## CHAPTER TAKE-AWAY: CLOSING THOUGHTS

- Some can occasionally have marketing success based on judgment, but over the long term, the odds (of suboptimal efficiency) will catch up to most of us. Thus, it is likely best to manage the odds, by using research and by learning from the databases.

- The best practices of advertising, marketing, and personal motivation follow the genetic evolutionary traits of mankind.

- Product management is about managing the product, but brand management is based on the concepts of emotional associations, brand attitudes, imagery, persona, artwork, naming, and so on. This is about leveraging the emotional payoffs and emotional gimmes that humans judge and seek: what are the emotional associations, extra sensory appeals, advertising properties, brand icons or characters, and emotional payoffs to consumers on their terms?

- Marketing is not just about creating an emotional response. The focus needs to be on emoti-suasion (the benefit) rather than emotional response (the fleeting reaction to a stimulus). Often ads that are emotionally soft and moody fail to be persuasive because they do a poor job of engaging the brain and credibly building emotional associations onto the brand.

- Differentiation or Domination? If emotions, personal values, and self-centered desires are the fundamental basis of our motivations, then perhaps brand managers should focus on the consumer and his or her emotional desires. It is less important to worry about brand characteristics, differentiation, and unique selling propositions (USPs). These are not consumers' interests! Consumers want it all, not just one benefit. Being vague and all-encompassing with brand positioning allows consumers to create their own relationships with the brand.

- Key questions to ask (to ask alone, void of biases from others) about new marketing or advertising concepts:
  1. What is the Big Idea? (A two-sentence description you could give to a stranger.)
  2. Is this a single, unified, simple Big Idea?
  3. Is it strategically focused and does it build emotional associations (payoffs)?
  4. Does it undeniably involve the brand, with strong brand integration?
  5. Is it original, different, or novel to be irregular?
  6. Is it campaignable (to build or leverage ad properties for future advertising)?
  7. Does it leverage the power of *because* with a license to believe?

**Attitudinal Brand Equity**—The attitudes, desires, feelings, and imagery associated with a brand.

**Behavioral Brand Loyalty**—The degree to which consumers buy a particular brand rather than buying competitive brands. This is based on actual past purchases.

**Brand Health**—The in-market success of a brand due to brand equity and to brand loyalty. Often this is reflected by strong desires to buy a brand, even if not low priced, with good profit margins and share trends.

**Frequency**—The average number of times consumers have been exposed to or had an opportunity to see the advertisement (reached). For example, 3.7 times (averaged across all of those reached).

**Off-Air**—The period(s) when the brand is *not* advertising to consumers.

**On-Air**—The period(s) when the brand is being advertised (in one or more media).

**Reach**—Percentage of the defined target that has had the chance to see the ad. For example, 25 percent of females 18 to 49 years of age. To be precise, reach does not describe the percentage of the audience who saw the ad, just the opportunity to see it (an OTS).

**Recency Media Planning**—Trying to expose an ad to each consumer as close as possible to when he or she makes a category purchase (just before). Since purchases are spread out all year long, and each consumer is a part of this sequence over the year, one needs to avoid off-air gaps, since this represents lost opportunity to intercept the consumer with an ad just before purchasing.

**Share of Voice**—Share of voice is the share of the total cumulative category advertising accounted for by a specific brand in a defined period (e.g., 30 percent of all the advertising dollars was for brand X in June). This can be defined as share for just one medium or across many.

**Targeted Rating Points (TRPs [TVRs in Europe])**—A summary score (units) for exposure to advertising, calculated as Reach × Frequency. For example, 25 percent reach × 3.7 times = 92.5 TRPs.

# BIBLIOGRAPHY

Cialdini, Robert B. *Influence: The Physiology of Persuasion.* New York: Quill, 1984.

Cigliano, J., M. Georgiadis, D. Pleasance, and S. Walley. The price of loyalty. *McKinsey Quarterly* 4 (2000): 68–77.

Damasio, A. R. *Descartes' Error.* New York, G.P. Putnam's Sons, 1994.

Dawkins, Richard. *The Selfish Gene.* New York: Oxford University Press, 1976.

Diamond, Jared. *Collapse: How Societies Choose to Fail or Succeed.* New York: Penguin, 2005

Ford, Kevin. *Brands Laid Bare.* West Sussex, England: Wiley, 2005.

Gladwell, Malcolm. *The Tipping Point.* Boston: Back Bay Books, 2000, 2002.

———. *Blink: The Power of Thinking Without Thinking.* New York: Little, Brown and Company, 2005.

Johnson, Spencer. *The One Minute Sales Person.* New York: Avon Books, 1986.

Jones, John Philip. *When Ads Work.* New York: Lexington Books, 1995.

Keiningham, Timothy L., Terry G. Vavra, Lerzan Aksoy, and Henri Wallard. *Loyalty Myths.* New Jersey: Wiley, 2005.

Laibson, David, S. M. McClure, J. D. Cohen, and George Loewenstein. Separate neural systems value immediate and delayed monetary rewards. *Science* October (2004): 503–15.

# BIBLIOGRAPHY

Levitt, Steven D., and Stephen J. Dubner. *Freakonomics*. New York: Harper-Collins, 2005.

Lindstrom, Martin. *Brand Sense*. New York: Free Press, 2005.

Wright, Robert. *The Moral Animal*. New York: Vintage Books, 1995.

Zaltman, Gerald. *How Customers Think*. Boston: Harvard Business School Press, 2003.

Ad*Graph, 5, 11–12, 66, 181, 184, 189, 190

Ad recall, 66–73, 167–176, 178–179, 191–192

Advertising. *See* Brand management; Marketing

Aleve, and appreciating consumer attitudes, 96

Apple, 21–22, 106

Aspirations, as motivation, 111–112, 153–157

Attitudes:
appreciating, 95–97, 137–139
changing, 94–97, 124
forming, 92–93
and future decision making, 93–94
overview, 91–92
targeting, 122–126
*See also* Emotions; Motivation

Audi, and brand imagery, 124

AVIS, and evolving marketing concepts, 178

Bayer Aspirin, 95–96

*Blink* (Gladwell), 83

Brand equity, 18, 19, 135–136, 142–146, 160–161. *See also* Brand management; Equity*Builder

Brand*Graph, 66

Brand icons, 23–24. *See also* Brand management, emotional appeal

Branding, 67–70, 134–136, 171, 172, 173–176

Brand management:
ad recall, 66–73, 167–176, 178–179, 192–193 (*see also* Memory; Senses)
ad repetition, 70–73 (*see also* Ad recall; Memory)
brand associations, 59–51, 64, 85–86, 154–158
brand attribution, 67–70, 71 (*see also* Ad recall)
branding as a concept, 134–136, 173–176

Brand management (*continued*)
  as a business, 131–133, 203–205
  challenges of, 4–15, 198–205
  and choices, 38–39
  commoditization, 7–8
  and the competition, 95–97
  consistency, 175–176
  and consumer attitudes (*see* Attitudes)
  and consumer motivation (*see* Motivation)
  copycat products, 6, 7
  and decision making, 38–40, 137–138
  desensitizing, 4–6, 57–58, 73'
  difficult research, 12–14
  and disloyal consumers, 8–9
  emotional appeal, 21–24, 124
  failed advertising, 10–12
  innovation, 20–21, 24–25, 139–140, 180–181
  and internet shopping, 9–10
  and irregularity, 37
  manufacturers vs. retailers, 7–8
  media fragmentation, 10
  overengineering, 24–25, 166–167
  price vs. value, 164–166
  price competition, 17–19
  purchase habits, 34–36
  and recency planning, 188–192, 208
  and science, 25–26
  substitutability, 6–7
  35 tools of, 137–194
  unified approach to, 181–184, 185–188
  using advertising pretests, 133–134

*See also* Attitudes; Brand equity; Emotions; Evolution
Brand physique, 23, 162. *See also* Brand management, emotional appeal
Buckley's Mixture, and consumer attitudes, 95
Bystander problem, 83–84

Cage, Phineas, 47, 82–83. *See also* Human brain
Cerebral cortex, 48, 50, 55–56, 88, 126. *See also* Emotions; Evolution; Human brain; Senses
Cialdini, Robert, 146–147, 178–179
Coca-Cola, 18, 96, 97, 134–135. *See also* Brand equity
Cognitive dissonance, 39–40
Cohen, J. D., 87
*Collapse* (Diamond), 200
Comfort zone, as motivation, 112
Commoditization of the category, 7–8
Corpus callosum, 48–49, 88, 126. *See also* Emotions; Human brain; Senses
Coupons, 18–19. *See also* Brand management, price competition

Damasio, Antonio, 83
Darwin, Charles, 29, 30–32
Dawkins, Richard, 9
Déjà vu, 49. *See also* Human brain
*Descartes' Error* (Damasio), 83
Desensitization, 32, 57
Diamond, Jared, 200
Differentiation, 6–7, 139–140, 171, 177–178, 202–203

Dubner, Stephen, 113
Duracell, 20
DVRs (digital video recorders), and
    ad repetition, 73
Dyslexia, 47–48. *See also* Human
    brain

eBay, 9
Economically rational man, 87–
    88
Expectancy theory, 118–120
Expedia, 9
Emotions:
    eleven emotional drivers, 157–160
    and irrational decision making,
        86–89, 147–152
    overview, 77–79
    and rational decision making,
        79–86, 88
    and targeting, 122–126
    *See also* Attitudes; Brand man-
        agement; Emoti-suasion;
        Motivation
Emoti*Scape, 148–152, 153
Emoti-suasion:
    concept of, xix, 200–205
    and consumer attitudes (*see* At-
        titudes)
    defined, xviii
    emotional associations, 24, 83
    examples of, xix, 12–14, 110–
        111, 119, 144
    and motivation (*see* Motivation)
    and science, 25–26
    triggering, 120–122
    *See also* Brand management,
        emotional appeal; Emotions;
        Evolution; Human brain, emo-
        tions in; Senses, entry of

Energizer, 20
Engrams, 44, 63, 64. *See also* Hu-
    man brain; Senses
Equity*Builder, 6–7, 135–136, 141,
    144–145, 161, 166. *See also*
    Brand equity
Evolution:
    cognitive dissonance, 39–40
    and decision making, 38–40,
        176–177
    and detecting irregularity,
        36–37, 177–178
    genetics, 32–33, 109
    and habits, 33–36
    vs. intelligent design, 32
    overview, 29–32, 198

Fast-moving consumer goods
    (FMCGs), 4
*Freakonomics* (Levitt), 113
Functional MRI (fMRI), 48

Georgiadis, M., 19
Gillette, 20, 25
Gladwell, Malcolm, 83, 121–122

Heath, Robert, 71. *See also* Low at-
    tribution processing (LAP)
Hedonism, as motivation, 110–
    111, 140–141, 158
*How Customers Think* (Zaltman),
    36, 54–55, 65
Human brain:
    areas of, 47–50
    emotions in, 51–52
    growth of, 50–51
    memory units (*see* Memory,
        units of)
    neurons, 44–47 (*see also* Memory)

Human brain (*continued*)
  workings of, 88
  *See also* Emotions; Evolution;
    Senses

Incentives, as motivation, 113–114
*Influence: The Psychology of Per-
  suasion* (Cialdini), 146–147,
  178–179
Intelligent design, 32
Iyengar, Sheena, 38

J. D. Power & Associates, 119
Johnson, Spencer, 105
Jones, John P., 187–188

Kay, John, 87–88
Kellogg's Raisin Bran, 120
Kia, and consumer attitudes, 93

Laibson, David, 87
Lepper, Mark, 38
Levanthal, Howard, 121–122
Levitt, Steven, 113
License-to-believe, as marketing
  concept, 180
Limbic system, 55–56, 83, 87, 88,
  126. *See also* Human brain;
    Senses
Listerine, and consumer attitudes,
  94
Lizard brain, 50, 55–56, 88. *See
  also* Cerebral cortex
Loewenstein, George, 87
Low attention processing (LAP),
  70–73
Loyalty programs, 19. *See also*
  Brand management, price
  competition

Magnetic resonance imaging
  (MRI), 48
Manipulation, xviii
Marketing:
  and consumer attitudes (see At-
    titudes)
  and consumer motivation (*see*
    Motivation)
  and consumer targeting, 122–125
  goal of, xvii
  role of, xviii
  *See also* Brand management
Maslow, Abraham, and hierarchy
  of needs, 100–103, 111
McClure, S. M., 87
McDonald's, and brand associations, 85–86, 92, 159–160
McKinsey & Company, 19
Memory:
  of advertising, 66–73
  overview, 46–47, 63–64
  short-term vs. long-term, 64,
    71–72, 87
  units of, 46–47, 65–66, 73–75
  *See also* Emotions; Human brain;
    Senses
Miller beer, and successful triggering, 120–121
Mnemonic, 65. *See also* Memory
*The Moral Animal* (Wright), 30–31,
  33
Motivation:
  aspirations, 111–112, 153–157
  authenticity, 102–103
  belonging, 103
  cognitive style, 103–106
  comfort zone, 112, 153–157
  desire, 103, 141–143, 157–159
  expectancy theory, 118–120

hedonism, 111–112, 140–141, 158
hierarchy of needs, 100–103,
  157–160
incentives, 113–114
necessity, 103
overview, 99–101, 117–118
popularity, 146–147
self-perception, 106–107,
  153–157
targeting, 122–126
triggering, 120–122, 146
*See also* Brand management;
  Emoti-suasion; Unique selling
  proposition (USP);
Myers-Briggs Type Indicator
  (MBTI), 104–105

Neuroscience. *See* Human brain;
  Senses
Next\*, 66
Next\*Idea, 133
Next\*TV, 133, 178
Nike, 21, 112. *See also* Brand man-
  agement, innovation

*The One Minute Salesperson* (Johnson), 105
*The Origin of Species* (Darwin), 29,
  30

Pepsi, and appreciating consumer
  attitudes, 96–97
Perrier, and brand physique, 162
Pleasance, D., 19
Pony Express, and commercial
  wear-out, 183
Popularity, 136, 146–147, 202
Powerball lottery, as incentive,
  113–114

Price reductions. *See* Brand management, price competition
Proctor & Gamble, 18, 20, 134–
  135, 165–166
Promotions, 18–19. *See also* Brand
  management, price competition

Recency planning, as marketing
  concept, 187–191, 208
Reward center, 56

*Science Matters* (Suzuki), 58
*The Selfish Gene* (Dawkins), 9
Self-perceptions, 106–107
Senses:
  deprivation, 58–59
  desesitizing, 57, 58
  entry of, 55–56, 161–163
  hearing, 88, 126, 163
  overview, 53–55, 161–164
  smell, 46, 53–54, 57, 63, 88, 126,
    163
  taste, 54, 57, 88, 126, 163
  touch, 57, 88, 126, 163
  vision, 49, 54, 63, 88, 126, 163
  *See also* Brand management,
    brand sensations; Human
    brain; Synaesthesia
Sensory deprivation, 58–59. *See
  also* Senses
Share of voice, 187, 208
Social proof, 146–147, 179–180
Split brains, 49. *See also* Human
  brain
Starbucks, and brand associations,
  22, 159–160
Stella Artois, as brand niche, 139–140
Stimuli, 55–58. *See also* Senses

Suzuki, David, 58
Synaesthesia, 49–50. *See also* Human brain

Thinking brain, 55–56. *See also* Human brain; Lizard brain; Senses
*The Tipping Point* (Gladwell), 121–122
Travelocity, 9
Triggering, 120–122, 146
Tropicana, 20
Tylenol, and appreciating consumer attitudes, 96

Unique selling proposition (USP), 202–203

Virgin, 21. *See also* Brand management, innovation
Volkswagen, and brand imagery, 124
Volvo, and successful targeting, 125
Vroom, Victor, 118

Walley, S., 19
Wal-Mart, 8, 17, 21
Wanamaker, John, 132
Wear-out, 183–184
*When Ads Work* (Jones), 187–188
Wright, Robert, 30–31, 33

Zaltman, Gerald, 36, 54–55, 65